Turn to

Dr. Spock's The First Two Years

for invaluable advice on topics vital to all new parents:

- The many meanings of your newborn's cries
- Separation anxiety
- Helping your child cope with unfamiliar faces
- Understanding baby's moods and emotions
- Sibling jealousy
- Sleep problems
- Dealing with the stresses of parenthood

. . . and more!

BOOKS BY BENJAMIN SPOCK, M.D.

Dr. Spock's Baby and Child Care
Dr. Spock on Parenting
Dr. Spock's The First Two Years
Dr. Spock's The School Years

Published by POCKET BOOKS

Dr. Spock's

THE
FIRST TWO
YEARS

The Emotional and Physical Needs
of Children from Birth to Age Two

Benjamin Spock, M.D.
edited by Martin T. Stein, M.D.

POCKET BOOKS
New York   London   Toronto   Sydney   Singapore

An *Original* Publication of POCKET BOOKS

 POCKET BOOKS, a division of Simon & Schuster, Inc.
1230 Avenue of the Americas, New York, NY 10020

ISBN: 0-7434-1122-6

First Pocket Books trade paperback printing August 2001

10 9 8 7 6 5 4 3 2 1

POCKET and colophon are registered trademarks of Simon & Schuster, Inc.

Book design by Helene Berinsky
Front cover photo by VCG/FPG International

Printed in the U.S.A.

This book is comprised of a series of essays previously published individually in *Redbook* (1985–1992) and *Parenting* (1992–1998).

For information regarding special discounts for bulk purchases, please contact Simon & Schuster Special Sales at 1-800-456-6798 or business@simonandschuster.com

This book is dedicated to

the mothers and fathers who taught Dr. Spock about the growth and emotional development of their children;

Dr. Benjamin Spock, who shared with me, during the last year of his remarkable life, the evolution of his ideas about the development of children;

Mary Morgan, Dr. Spock's widow, who steadfastly maintains his legacy for the children and parents of future generations;

my parents, Gertrude and Gerald Stein, who guided the lives of their children with a respect for their independence and an intuitive understanding of Dr. Spock's reminder to parents to "trust yourself . . . you know more than you think you do"; and

my wife, Mary Caffery, and children, Joshua, Benjamin and Sarah, who continue to teach me about the developmental journey of children and young adults.

Acknowledgments

There are many individuals who are important in the development of this book. I am indebted to the pediatricians who shaped my thinking about children, families, and the practice of pediatrics, including Drs. John Castiglione, Louis Fraad, William Nyhan, Samuel Spector, Stanford Friedman, John Kennell, and T. Berry Brazelton. I especially want to thank my colleague, Dr. Suzanne Dixon, with whom I collaborated during a twenty-year period at the University of California San Diego.

There are many other colleagues in the emerging specialty of Developmental and Behavioral Pediatrics who continue to work with me and teach me about ways to assist pediatricians to become more effective in counseling parents and the early recognition and treatment of children with develpmental and behavioral conditions. They include Drs. Michael Reiff, Heidi Feldman, Ellen Perrin, Paul Dworkin, William Coleman, Lane

Tanner, Jim Perrin, Mark Wolraich, Esther Wender, William Carey, Ronald Barr, Randi Hagerman, Barbara Howard, Robert Needlman, and David Snyder. My colleagues in San Diego, Philip Nader, Laurel Leslie, Barbara Loundsbury, Dorothy Johnson, Eyla Boies, and Howard Taras continue to support this work.

I also wish to express sincere appreciation to Robert Lescher, Dr. Spock's literary agent for many years. He steadfastly encouraged and guided the publication of this book. Dr. Spock wrote the original articles included in this book for two magazines for parents. Bruce Raskin encouraged and guided the publication as Dr. Spock's editor at *Parenting* magazine. Sylvia Koner was his editor at *Redbook*. I am also grateful to Tracy Bernstein, a superb editor at Pocket Books.

Dr. Benjamin Spock's legacy is sustained today at drSpock.com, a company that disseminates his writings and contemporary information for parents. The leadership of that group worked with me and actively encouraged the development of this book. I appreciate the support from Douglas Lee, John Buckley, David Markus, George Strait, and Drs. Laura Janna, Robert Needlman, and Lynn Cates.

Contents

Introduction

For nearly sixty years, from the 1940s to the end of the twentieth century, Dr. Benjamin Spock was *the* pediatrician to whom parents turned for guidance about a wide variety of child-rearing issues. The popularity of his first book, *Baby and Child Care,* brought national and international recognition to Dr. Spock for his sound, practical advice and gentle voice. It became the most widely read book on child care ever written.

Today, decades later, it is still the most respected parenting book in the world; and Dr. Spock's other books have been equally celebrated. Although he is gone, millions of parents continue to "consult" him by virtue of his writings. Why such popularity and success? I think there are three major reasons.

First, his range of subjects was comprehensive, addressing parents' concerns about both physical health (for example, nutrition, safety, immunizations, early signs of illness, and home remedies) and psychological health (normal development, parent and sibling relationships, the different experiences of mothers and fathers, the effects of work outside the home on family life, and many others).

Second, a hallmark of his writing is that Dr. Spock "spoke" to parents. Mothers and fathers often wrote to him with some variation of "When I read your book, it is as if you are sitting at my kitchen table talking and listening to me." His focus was always on the parent; he wrote with the assumption that parents are capable, wise, and open to understanding the development and needs of their children. "Trust yourself" was a theme that guided all of his advice to parents.

The third reason, I believe, for the preeminent place Dr. Spock continues to hold among parents is his respect for change and diversity. He recognized that the way we raise children reflects a culture's values, and that some of our values and perspectives on children and family change over time. Characteristically, he did not tell us "the right way to do it." He recognized the inherent value of diversity in families and communities. In every position he took, he respected that diversity.

This book derives from a series of articles published in two magazines, *Redbook* (1985–1992) and *Parenting* (1992–1998). The articles have been edited, catalogued, and published in two volumes.

Dr. Spock's The First Two Years addresses the major concerns of new parents, from planning for the arrival of a new baby to problems with sleep, toilet training, and temper tantrums in the second year. The first chapter introduces the idea that babies have a remarkable ability to communicate with parents and others immediately after birth, and aims to improve our ability to respond to and interact with them. In the second chapter, Dr. Spock answers specific concerns raised by parents, from a floppy, misshapen head after birth to a baby's breathing patterns, jaundice, spitting-up, and Sudden Infant Death Syndrome (SIDS).

From his experience in pediatric practice, Dr. Spock recognized the importance of quality communication and trust between parents and a child's doctor. In the section "Choosing a doctor for your baby" he encourages both parents and doctors to work at building this alliance and provides some specific guidelines.

The next section is a how-to-guide that covers feeding (breast and formula feeding), baby equipment for the home, preparing the older sibling for the arrival of the new baby, and circumcision. Infant nutrition is then discussed in detail, followed by a section on teething, colds, and ear infections. In each case, Dr. Spock helps parents to see the emotional side of a new experience for a baby, from the introduction of solid foods and weaning from breast milk (or a bottle) to teething and colds.

Special attention is given to developmental events in the first two years that may have an impact on parent-child relationships, including the baby's response to a stranger, the use of a comforter (including pacifiers and thumb sucking), sleep variations, and toilet training. The final chapters on discipline, temper tantrums, and spoiling explore perhaps the most challenging moments of parenting in the second year of life.

The second book, *Dr. Spock's The School Years*, explores current trends in our society that affect families, including the effects of media violence on children and teens, parents' work outside the home, child care, peer pressure, adolescent sexuality, and many more. The complete table of contents can be found at the end of this volume.

During the year prior to his recent death, Dr. Spock and I met several times each week. With his wife, Mary Morgan, he had moved from the colder climate of his beloved Maine to southern California, a more gentle climate at a time of declining health. Sitting in his patio surrounded by many plants, colorful flowers, a large aquarium and a canyon view covered with green chaparral, we talked about children. Together, we reviewed the seventh edition of *Baby and Child Care*. I was amazed at his enthusiasm. At ninety-four years of age, with a weakening physical body, he found the intellectual and emotional strength to engage and be engaged in a dialogue about ideas that remained important to him. Ways to encourage and sustain breast-feeding, eliminating the traditional use of powder for diaper rashes, aspects of his new recommendation for a vegetarian diet, and new approaches to problems with bed-wetting are just a few of the subjects we discussed. Dr. Spock's thoughtful responses were consistently laced with his clinical experiences and the ideas and suggestions he gleaned from the many parents who wrote to him.

When I read the essays collected in this book I hear that voice. It is a voice that comes from an informed and thoughtful mind, a voice that speaks directly to parents—with confidence in your wish to be a good parent. He trusted and respected your intelligence and good intentions. It is my hope that this book captures the knowledge and wisdom of a superb pediatrician who dedicated his life to the emotional and physical health of children.

THE
FIRST TWO
YEARS

1

Communicating with Your Baby:

READING YOUR BABY'S CUES

Babies can express their feelings and needs in many ways. Learning to read your baby is very important, especially for parents who want to respond to their baby's needs appropriately. Crying is a major source of communication that the newborn baby has. So in one way, it's a very healthy sign that your baby can cry and let you know that he needs you. The bond between the parent and baby may be deepened if parents are sensitive to their baby's cries, gestures, and behavior in general.

I feel that it is very important to learn to listen to your children. You can learn to listen to your baby even at its very early age. Listening means focusing your attention, not in a worried way, but in an observing manner. You want to learn what your baby wants and needs. You can read books and articles but the main way you will learn about your baby is to be observant in a meaningful way. That means spending time looking and listening to your baby, not just feeding and cleaning him, and putting him to sleep, but also keenly focusing your undivided attention to him. And then trusting yourself. Because you *do* know more than you think you do.

Crying: An Early Form of Communication with Parents

The first signal you'll get from your baby may be a cry. In the early weeks this will probably come when the baby is hungry and later will include not only being hungry, but also being wet, or uncomfortable. If your baby cries during the first few weeks, then you can respond by feeding her without a fear of spoiling her. She may be hungry before her feeding time, but that's okay. In the early weeks, the baby will need to feed often and may or may not go by any set schedule. Let your baby be the guide as to how often she needs to feed.

She may also cry if she is uncomfortable and needs to burp after a feeding. You can gently pat her on her back as you put her over your shoulder to see if she can burp up any air she may have swallowed during feeding. You should trust your own instincts, and watch for a pattern in the baby's crying. You will soon learn to "read" your baby's cry, and distinguish a cry of hunger from a cry of pain.

Some babies cry more during the day, others at night, and some cry without regard for the time of the day or night. Patterns of crying among individual babies often reflect the baby's own "temperament"— her emotional reaction to a new situation, her activity level, and attention to people and things around her. Many of her emotional responses are a reflection of the way her unique brain has been "wired" to respond to different situations. I have found that many parents learn to respond to their baby with greater comfort when they know about different patterns of crying.

Baby Colic

When a baby cries regularly in the late afternoon, or evening, and cries about the same time everyday, we call it colic. Most colicky babies cry for over three hours in each twenty-four hour period. The colicky baby appears to be in pain with a distended tummy and gas. Colic usually starts at about two to four weeks of age and will last during the first three months, then will go away. The crying in *some* colicky babies begins after the feeding when they may have been either overfed or underfed. Extended crying before the feeding is seen with a hungry baby. A baby with colic gains weight at the expected rate and has a normal examination. Colic can occur in both breast-fed and bottle-fed babies.

Most parents feel very guilty and think they are doing something wrong. When your baby's clinician has examined your colicky infant and found nothing abnormal, you can be assured that your baby is healthy.

Changing the formula rarely helps. Use of caffeine drinks or lots of chocolate by a nursing mother may cause excessive crying; eliminating these foods decreases the crying. Occasionally, the colic may be a sensitivity to proteins from cow's milk consumed by a nursing mother; before eliminating milk in their diet, nursing mothers should consult their baby's clinician. In many cases, offering a pacifier will be helpful. And you may find that the baby is more comfortable on her stomach. Other colicky babies seem to be comfortable being picked up, held, rocked calmly and quietly, or being placed in a crib with a light blanket wrapped comfortably around the body. Some babies are colicky as a result of too much stimulation in the home. Less noise, quiet soothing music and being careful not to overstimulate your baby will be helpful. The soothing noise of a hair dryer or vacuum cleaner placed near the baby's crib will settle some colicky babies.

Remember, you don't have to be afraid of spoiling the baby by picking her up at this age. An older child may become demanding at a later age, and use crying as a way to manipulate his parents to get what he wants. But a young baby during the first three months of age is *not* spoiled when he cries. He is crying because he needs something, not because he wants to control his parents. (That comes at a later age.) You can take a baby's early cries as a genuine cry of distress and discomfort, and respond without any fear that you might be spoiling him.

Periodic Irritable Baby

A baby who regularly cries at a certain time of day (usually late afternoon or evening), and is not distended (as is the colicky baby), is called a periodic irritable baby. Usually this crying will correct itself after three months of age. The baby does not seem to be in pain, and her cries are usually less painful than with colic, but still at a regular time.

You may find that the periodic irritable baby can benefit from being held, or walked, or rocked. She may be comforted by another feeding. Or simply a pacifier in her mouth will give her comfort.

Fretful Baby

A fretful baby is one which is fussy off and on during the day or night. She doesn't cry at any regular hour, she doesn't seem to be in pain, and usually her tummy is not distended. Your fretful baby may have a harder time adjusting to a schedule. Usually they fuss the first three months, but soon become adjusted to the outside world and calm down later. It seems their nervous system as well as young digestive system have a period of adjustment the first three months.

• • •

Cries of Hunger

Hunger is the most common cause of crying in the early months. The baby has no other way to communicate his needs to eat except to cry. He may be hungry if he nursed at only one breast or took only half of his formula during the last feeding. He may wake up crying if he has outgrown his formula or his mother's milk and needs more to eat as he grows. He may want to be fed more often during certain hours.

You may be on a regular four-hour schedule or you may be feeding according to his desires. In any case, you should not try to feed the baby every time he cries. Try to wait a few minutes, or use a pacifier, if it's just two hours or less since the last feeding. If it's been longer than two hours, or if the last feeding was incomplete, then you may want to feed sooner.

Hypertonic Baby

A hypertonic baby is very jumpy and doesn't relax well. This baby is bothered by sudden movements, loud noises, and sometimes is very uncomfortable in a tub bath. She may also have symptoms of colic or periodic irritable crying. If you suspect your baby is a hypertonic one, then she may be comforted by swaddling her in a receiving blanket. She will enjoy a sponge bath more than a tub bath. And you will want to keep the noise down. And have few visitors and the least amount of sudden movement for her.

Crying Associated with Diaper Rash and Teething

Some babies with more sensitive skin will cry when they are wet, especially if they have a sore bottom or a rash. If you think that your baby's crying starts up when she is wet, the diaper may be changed as soon as the baby wets it. Even disposable diapers, although they are more absorbent than cloth diapers, should be changed to prevent skin irritation if you discover that your baby settles after a change.

When fretfulness and crying are associated with drooling and biting, your baby is communicating signs of teething. The behaviors associated with the eruption of baby teeth may take place from the age of three or four months until two and one-half years of age. The baby will want to put things in his mouth: his fist, his toys, or anything he can put his hands on.

It's good to recognize the signs of teething because it goes on for several years. Healthy babies respond to teething in dramatically different ways. Some babies manage teething without much fretfulness. Others may be very wakeful during teething.

You might want to provide some safe chewable objects such as rubber teething rings. (Be careful that the toys you provide aren't thin brittle plastic which can break off and be swallowed.) You may find that rubbing the baby's gums is soothing. Some teething can also cause loss of appetite and crying during the night. A brief nursing can sometimes put the baby back to sleep.

Responding to Your Baby's Cry: A Few Specific Suggestions

There are a variety of ways you may want to respond to your baby's cry. Babies are different in their response to different interventions by parents. Through practice, you will learn about your baby's response to different kinds of treatments at home.

1. Go to the baby and pick her up. And you can do so without fear of spoiling at this early age.

2. You may already know that she is hungry, and offer her the breast or bottle. If she has just recently had a feeding, you may offer her a pacifier and postpone the feeding for a while.

3. Some babies will benefit from walking or gentle rocking and go back to sleep. Others will calm down if they are wrapped or swaddled in a blanket.

4. Some parents take the baby for a walk in the stroller or a ride in the car.

5. If the baby seems in pain, then you can try placing her on your knees and use a gentle jouncing.

6. If you are very careful to use warm and *not* hot water, you can place the baby on a *warm* water bottle with a diaper or towel for protection.

7. You may use music or sing to a fussy baby.

Though no research has yet revealed the cause of fretfulness or colic, speculation has focused lately on the contrast between traditional societies in developing countries in which there is nearly constant bodily contact between mother and infant and very little crying, and our industrial society in which the infant is insulated from mother in a crib and, as far as possible, from sounds, in a separate room. This suggests that parents should not be worrying about spoiling in the first three months but should try carrying the fretful or colicky baby in a canvas or cloth carrier, or swinging her in a mechanical swing or be treating her to music, not just when fussing but during much of the day.

It's best if you don't exhaust yourself. Your baby may be fatigued also. Just remember that babies usually grow out of this crying period after the first three months. And you shouldn't blame yourself, or feel guilty, if your baby has any of these crying characteristics. You should be better able to understand your baby's cries after some careful listening and more experience.

Is the Baby Sick?

Usually a baby can become very irritable just before coming down with a cold or an infection of some kind. You can take the baby's temperature, and if there is a fever, then report this to your doctor. The baby may have a runny nose, a cough, loose bowel movements, vomiting, or other symptoms. This crying is different since it has these other symptoms to go along with it. You should watch your baby closely for any changes in the stools, or changes in temperature, or changes in eating habits. You should report all of these symptoms to your doctor, who will advise you as to how to take care of your baby.

Sucking

Babies love to suck. They suck not only for feeding, but for the pure joy of sucking. You may observe this vigorous response immediately after birth when a baby is breast-fed while its mother is still on the delivery table.

The best way to satisfy your baby's sucking needs is to provide a long enough feeding time to satisfy not only hunger, but also the need to suck. Breast-feeding usually takes care of this problem if the baby is allowed to nurse until he is satisfied. Usually twenty minutes is enough time to satisfy both hunger as well as sucking needs. If you bottle-feed, make sure the holes in the nipples are not so large that the baby finishes the milk in say ten minutes, but hasn't had a chance to satisfy his sucking needs.

Sucking helps babies relieve physical as well as emotional tension and can calm a fretful baby. Sucking the thumb sometimes helps a baby satisfy this need and should not be denied. You might have seen your baby suck her thumb at the time of an ultrasound examination during pregnancy! Some parents find a pacifier is satisfying and will discourage thumb sucking. And the pacifier can more easily be given up at age three to four months than thumb sucking. There are some fussy babies who seem more alert and tranquil when sucking a pacifier during the first year of life.

If you are nursing and choose to offer your baby a pacifier, wait a week or two until the baby has learned to nurse effectively. When some nursing babies are given a pacifier in the first few days after birth, they may find it difficult to learn to suck at the breast.

Reaching Out

If your baby reaches out for you, then she probably wants you to pick her up—and this doesn't mean that you are spoiling her. She needs to have contact with you during these early months by picking her up, holding her, *gently* rocking her, talking to her, or walking her.

If she holds her arms out to you, with or without crying, she needs to be responded to—and all parents will want to respond to the outreaching arms of their baby. Sometimes this reaching out may come in the middle of changing a soiled diaper, and this could delay your response somewhat. But this is only temporary and won't cause her to become upset if the baby knows that you will eventually respond to her.

Kicking Legs

If your baby is kicking his legs in glee in the bath, and smiling and cooing, then you can rest assured the baby is enjoying his bath. Your response can be to continue his bath and let him play in water. Some babies kick when they feel excited, such as anticipation of the upcoming feeding. Usually the kicking is also joined by hand waving and head movements.

Some kicking also may occur when the baby is crying or fretful. I'd say the kicking alone is not enough to say what kind of response is necessary. It would depend on what else is going on with the baby. Is she crying and kicking, or smiling and kicking? Does she enjoy kicking? If so, then no response is necessary.

Grunting

Some signals or signs may have no particular meaning, or mean different things at different times, depending on what else is going on with the baby at that particular moment.

For example, most babies make grunting sounds occasionally. These are squeaks or throat-clearing sounds. She may be listening to her own sound and enjoying it. She may be imitating your voice. She may be grunting with pleasure. At another time her grunts may be with stomach pain or a wet diaper. I think in this case you would want to see how your baby is in general—not just go by the grunt alone. She will have an expression on her face which also should give you a clue. And she may grunt in her sleep, as if she were dreaming; or she may happily grunt when she is awake and anticipates being fed. Each time would mean a different response from you, depending on the circumstance. At about two months of age, she will develop a cooing sound which comes from the back of her throat; this is the first real sign of her learning to use language.

High-pitched Squealing

When babies first realize they can make a sound, they may repeat it over and over with glee realizing they have made this wonderful new noise. Some babies will make a high-pitched squealing sound, and listen to see if they can do it again. The high-pitch seems to excite them, and what makes it more exciting is when the parents respond. A happy baby can entertain themselves endlessly by producing these early pre-language sounds. These sounds often do not require a response. Some parents enjoy repeating the sound themselves to keep the baby company in her search for verbalizing in a nonverbal way. Just noticing and talking back, and showing your appreciation is enough in most cases.

The Parent's Response

Most parents are thrilled when their babies begin giving signs of being more grown-up. After weeks of mostly sleeping and eating, your baby will begin making sounds and gestures that may indicate the baby's disposition.

The main thing to remember is that any response that you give is appreciated by the baby. When parents smile, talk, and pick up the baby, then the baby learns to give more of these signs and develops others. The main thing is to give attention in a loving and kind manner, rather than focusing on how to analyze every squirm. The analysis of every signal is less important. The fact that you are there and that you are eager and excited about your baby's behavior, and you show it in your expressions and tone of voice, is more important. If you are too worried about how to figure out every grunt or gesture, your worry will overshadow your warmth, tenderness, kindness, and excitement. Your enthusiasm to any response will be more valuable than the exact "what exactly did you mean by that?"

Happy to Crying

Babies can go from being happy one minute to crying the next. And they can stop crying and be happy again just as quickly. Their moods can vary from one moment to the next. It's good to know that your baby's sadness at one moment can be changed so fast if you observe and see why she is sad. Some babies will be happy the second they feel relief from their hunger. Others can be screaming one moment, and instantly stop as soon as you pick them up. They have a tendency to turn on the sobs when they can't communicate any other way. But they are easily satisfied as soon as you respond appropriately. If they can switch so easily from one mood to another, then you can take advantage of this, knowing she will forgive you easily for putting her down to change a diaper. As soon as you respond, she will give you instant feedback if your response has been the right one.

Enjoy Your Baby

The main thing to remember is to enjoy your baby. All of the cooing, grunting, pre-verbal sounds, and other means of communication are wonderful ways to enjoy your baby. You can easily instill in her a sense of self-enjoyment by showing your own enjoyment at all that she does. A baby will get the sense that she is worth noticing and is loved. She will feel good about herself and gain self-confidence even at this early age, if you give her the response that she needs. Just being there for her is the first and best response. The more you are with her, the more you will learn how to read out her signals and respond accordingly.

2

Parents' Biggest Newborn Concerns

Since the first edition of *Baby and Child Care*, many parents have written to me about specific concerns during the newborn period. This is an unsettling time for all families, especially after the birth of a first newborn. With fewer parents of young children now living near their own parents or other relatives, many of the physical and emotional aspects of caring for a baby are no longer taught to new parents. It is for these reasons that I try to answer each question in clear and practical terms.

CONCERN: My baby's umbilical stump is pretty red and scary looking. Is it infected?

The umbilical stump forms when the cord, that connected your placenta and your baby in the womb, was cut at the time of birth. It takes from one to three weeks for the stump to heal and fall off. At times, you might see a small discharge as the stump heals. Occasionally, a pink area will develop over the baby's skin that is irritated by the cord. These are normal findings. You don't have to be concerned. If you notice that the skin around the cord is bright red, smell a harsh odor around the cord, or see a thick discharge of fluid, contact your baby's doctor. These are signs of an infection which needs prompt medical attention.

Most babies will not develop an infection of the umbilical stump if the area is kept clean and dry. Some doctors recommend the use of rubbing alcohol on a cotton swab twice each day until the cord heals. When bathing the baby during the healing process, do not let the bath water touch the stump. Sponge bathing with a damp cloth is sufficient, and keeping it dry also promotes healing and prevents infection. Your baby's "red and scary-looking" stump should receive immediate medical attention; however, most of these are found not to be infected when examined carefully by your baby's doctor or nurse practitioner.

CONCERN: When I took my baby home from the hospital, I was alarmed that her head was so floppy. What can I do about it?

All newborn babies have floppy heads. This is because the muscles around the neck that eventually support the head take time to strengthen after birth. Also, the baby's head is large in proportion to the rest of the body. This adds to the floppy appearance. The important thing to remember is that a floppy head and neck are normal in all babies. By two months of age, the muscles strengthen with development and control of the head is secure. Until then, you can support the baby's head comfortably with your arm when you hold him in a cradle position or with your free hand when holding your baby over your shoulder.

CONCERN: How do I prevent SIDS?

Sudden Infant Death Syndrome (SIDS) is a rare condition where a baby, usually under six months of life and healthy, is found dead in a crib. The cause is not known but we think that it is a result of poor coordination between the brain's control center for breathing and the baby's lungs. The good news is that we know a few things that will decrease your baby's risk for SIDS. Freeing the home of smoking, feeding the baby breast milk, and placing the infant on her back when in the crib have been shown to decrease the incidence of SIDS. None of these preventive measures were known when I first wrote *Baby and Child Care*. Careful research by pediatricians has brought hope to parents that many cases of SIDS are preventable. It's amazing that simply changing the position of the baby in the crib, from a tummy down position to a back position, has reduced the number of infants with SIDS by one-half! We once worried that a baby on her back would be at risk for spitting-up and choking. But, in fact, this is not a problem for most babies and I now recommend "back-to-sleep" as the safest position. If your infant has a condition in which excessive spitting or vomiting occurs, check with your baby's doctor about the best sleeping position.

CONCERN: How can I avoid exposing my baby to germs when visitors come to the house?

All parents try to prevent infections in their baby. Although you can't prevent every infection from spreading to your baby, there are some common-sense things you can do. Ask potential visitors to your home who have a cold, flu, or other contagious illness to postpone the visit until they are well. They will appreciate your concern for the baby and visit at another time. It's a good idea for all visitors and caretakers to wash their hands before holding a baby, especially in the first two months of life when your baby is more susceptible to infections. Young children, who are enchanted when they play and talk to babies, are more likely to have colds and be contagious. Children, by nature, are less inhibited with sneezing and coughing when around others. Their innocence makes them no less contagious. I say all this without wishing that you isolate your baby from relatives and friends. Certainly, babies need stimulation and parents need a break at times from the demands of child care. But these suggestions for limiting exposure to germs should lead to a balance between isolation and family social activities.

CONCERN: Is my baby getting enough breast milk? How can I know if she is getting enough? Also, is irregular feeding and milk intake a problem?

There are lots of ways to be assured that your baby receives enough breast milk. If your baby appears satisfied after nursing and sleeps contentedly following feeding, she has probably taken in an adequate amount of milk. Persistent crying and difficulty latching onto your breast may indicate poor intake. After the first few days of life after your milk has come in, the diaper should be wet from urine about six times each day. Urine from a well-fed baby is colorless or slightly yellow. Dark colored urine, a scant amount of urine, or a pink tinged urine (from crystal) *may* indicate inadequate intake of milk. Most nursing babies after the first week will have from three to ten bowel movements each day; a few will have one every other day. "Breast milk stools" are loose and a mustard-yellow color. Infrequent bowel movements or very small stools are signs of insufficient milk intake. A sudden decrease in urine or stool means a decrease in milk.

One of the most important aspects of a well baby visit is a check on your baby's weight. If you are concerned that your baby is not getting enough breast milk, don't hesitate to call your doctor or nurse practitioner and arrange for a weight check at the office. Another way to be sure about the baby's milk intake is to check if your breasts feel fuller before a feeding and softer immediately after nursing. Some mothers find it helpful to actually hear the baby swallow during a feeding and to observe milk in the baby's mouth.

Most healthy babies do not feed on a strict schedule. In the first few weeks of life, many babies do well with feedings every two hours for some periods during the day. Once your milk is in and your baby is nursing well, most babies will feed approximately every three to four hours. Patterns of nursing are variable from baby to baby. What is more important is that your baby appears content, the number of wet diapers and stools are adequate, and that weight gain is satisfactory. When this occurs, your baby will be thriving.

CONCERN: Why is a newborn's head so swollen, as if she's gone ten rounds in a heavyweight boxing match?

The journey through the birth canal is a slow process. To your baby (and you) it may seem endless. Since the head of a newborn baby is very large compared to its body size, the head is molded during the delivery. Newborns often appear with heads in the shape of a football. It's remarkable to see how quickly head shape returns to normal within one or two weeks. This "molding" of the head does not have any adverse effect on the brain or other aspects of your baby's health. Less commonly, a swelling on the back of the head, usually on only one side, may persist for a few weeks after birth. This happens when a small blood clot forms beneath the scalp skin during delivery. Similar to molding, it is not harmful and the odd shape of the head returns to normal.

CONCERN: My baby's breathing changes from time to time. Sometimes it sounds too labored and other times too soft. When should I worry?

The breath sounds of a newborn baby normally change at different times of the day and night. You probably notice these changes when your baby is sleeping. It is common to hear the breath sounds suddenly increase in rate for several minutes before returning to normal. Many healthy babies have this breathing pattern.

At another time when your baby's nose is congested, the breath sounds may be louder than normal. In this case, if the baby is otherwise comfortable and its skin color is normal, there is no need for concern. Occasional sneezing is also common and normal in your baby. Hiccups often alarm parents because they are loud and may go on for a long time. Most babies will go through periods of hiccups at some time without any adverse effect on their health. Hiccups and sneezing should be considered as normal entitlements of life!

When a baby's breathing rate is rapid and noisy and this pattern is sustained for many minutes, the baby may have a respiratory infection. Sometimes, this is associated with a pulling-inward of the muscles between the ribs. If your baby has any of these signs, consult your baby's doctor or nurse practitioner immediately.

CONCERN: Can I cause my baby brain damage by pressing too hard on her soft spot?

The soft spot on the top of your baby's head (also called the "fontanel") is the place where four bones that make up the front part of the head come together. It takes a year or more for these bones to grow together at which time your baby no longer has a soft spot. This area is not sensitive and you can't damage your baby's brain by touching it during bathing, changing clothes, or play. It's best to treat the soft spot like any other part of the body—with loving care.

CONCERN: If I tug too hard or lift my baby up by her arms, can I cause a dislocation?

Playing with your baby in a physical way that is safe and enjoyable is always encouraged. A dislocation of an arm joint in a newborn rarely occurs. However, there are a couple of maneuvers of the arms that may cause a temporary dislocation at the elbow. It is usually limited to children between three months and three years old. The most frequent cause of the elbow dislocation is seen when a parent is walking with a toddler and holding on by one hand. The child becomes distracted or upset and the parent innocently pulls the arm causing the dislocation. The affected limb is held straight down and motionless. Attempts to move the arm causes pain. In an infant, the same thing can be caused by a quick tug of the arm. Although only some children are susceptible to an elbow dislocation, it is best not to test your child!

Whenever a young child is not moving a limb in the usual way, a medical evaluation is indicated. Your child's doctor will diagnose this condition quickly and, in most cases, will relocate the elbow by a simple maneuver of the arm.

CONCERN: My baby spits up a lot. Sometimes I'm not sure if she is vomiting or just spitting up. What's the difference?

All babies spit up some of their milk some of the time. This is because the ring of muscle that tightens the entrance to the stomach takes time to mature. It should not worry you if your baby is healthy in other ways. By six months of age, most babies cease spitting. When spitting up or regurgitation is frequent and in large amounts, it is called "reflux." Although reflux is often messy and frustrating to parents, it is usually associated with a healthy and thriving baby. When your doctor confirms that reflux is the cause of frequent spitting up, she may suggest smaller, frequent feedings, thickening a meal with cereal, and after a feeding, briefly placing the baby on her tummy, with her head and chest slightly elevated, to empty the stomach quicker.

Vomiting refers to more forceful loss of stomach contents. When a baby vomits, the meal is usually brought up with such force that the food is projected forward ("projectile vomiting"). Vomiting is usually of more concern than spitting up. It can be caused by an infection, an obstruction of the intestines, and by other diseases. Vomiting in an infant should be evaluated by a physician if it persists or is associated with other symptoms such as lethargy, poor feeding, fever, or if the vomit contains blood.

CONCERN: With babies being sent home so soon from the hospital, how can I tell if jaundice is setting in? What do I do if my baby develops jaundice?

Many newborn babies develop a yellow tinge to their skin called jaundice. It is usually due to the baby's liver when it is immature in the first few days after birth. It starts on the upper part of the body and in some cases progresses down to the legs. Jaundice is rarely a serious problem; it usually resolves by the second week. Some babies develop jaundice as a result of insufficient milk intake; it may be an early clue to an inadequate intake of breast milk. Jaundice that covers most of the baby's body from the head to the legs may be due to differences in mother and infant blood types, infection, or a problem with the liver. Your baby's doctor may want to watch the degree of jaundice with a simple blood test which measures the chemical responsible for the jaundice.

3

Choosing a Doctor for Your Baby

It may turn out that you, the parent, will consult your child's doctor more than any other physician during your own life. Therefore, it's important to choose the kind of person who will suit you; or if you find that you've made an unsatisfactory choice, that you'll be able to improve the existing relationship with a frank discussion; or, if that doesn't work either, that you'll be able to change doctors with some success this time.

Different parents have different needs in a doctor for their children. And any one doctor can't hope to satisfy all parents. One mother has confidence only in an older physician with an air of wisdom. Another mother is intimidated by a distinguished seeming professional person. She's much more comfortable with a young, informal doctor with whom she quickly feels a friendly relationship. One parent wants a physician who specifies treatment in exact detail. Another can't stand that kind of fussiness; she likes casual directions that show the physician's confidence in her judgment. One mother wants a man, another a woman.

Much depends, first of all, on whether there are two or more doctors in your community, or in your health management organization, to give you a choice. If not, and if you find you're dissatisfied, you've got to screw up your courage and have a frank talk. In many such situations, the frank talk solves the difficulties well enough to make a go of the relationship. One thing to remember is that you and your baby's doctor aren't the first to have difficulty understanding and working with each other. Also, frankness in discussion of such difficulties may create, in the end, a better than average doctor-parent relationship.

Pediatrician or family doctor? A pediatrician is trained to care for the special needs of children and teenagers. The medical education of a pediatrician focuses on child development, the prevention of illness and the physical and emotional problems that are unique to children. In a majority of communities, especially if you live in a small town, there are no pediatricians. But this doesn't mean that the baby can't have expert care. A family doctor who regularly takes care of children can do an entirely satisfactory job treating a great majority of children's illnesses and the other problems of that age period. The important factors are whether the physician is familiar with the common conditions that she's called on to treat, and whether she is a thoughtful, helpful person. If a rare disease that's difficult to diagnose or treat appears, he or she can get a consultation with a specialist in another nearby city.

Nowadays there are especially trained pediatric nurse practitioners and also physician's assistants who work in physicians' offices, take histories, do physical examinations, give advice about everyday problems and management such as infant feeding. They have almost as much experience in these matters as the physician and can always get a prompt consultation from the physician when needed.

Today most families have medical insurance that includes the children and they all belong to a health management organization (HMO) or other group health plan that pays the bills and has many regulations. You must use one of the pediatricians or family doctors on their panel of the HMO if you want them to pay the bills. Most families find this arrangement much more satisfactory than the traditional fee for services, especially when serious illness strikes.

How do you start looking for a doctor for your baby? If there is only a family doctor in the community, he will probably deliver the baby and then become its doctor. If there is one doctor who specializes in obstetrics and another who is a family doctor or a pediatrician, there is no choice. However, if there are several physicians who practice pediatrics or family medicine and who serve a medical group in which the rest of your family belongs, you will be able to choose your child's physician. If your obstetrician is a sympathetic soul with whom you have a good relationship, discuss your preferences with him. But if you feel he wouldn't understand, you can turn to a woman friend.

People who don't have medical insurance and who feel they cannot afford it, can get good preventive health care at the city or county well-baby clinic. A way to secure health care advice at home during the early weeks of the baby's life is through a public health nurse or a visiting nurse association. If you don't have medical insurance through your job, Medicaid, or a private plan, ask about the Healthy Families program. It may provide your child with medical insurance at a low cost.

Suppose your child develops a disease or problem that worries you a lot and you don't feel entirely satisfied with your regular doctor's treatment or directions. You don't need to leave him or her unless you want to take this opportunity to do so. You can tell the doctor about your concern and ask for a consultation. This may embarrass you because it's to some degree an expression of lack of confidence. But it's a long standing tradition. And though it may be possible to make your doctor unhappy, he or she should be able to accept it in a cooperative professional spirit. And the more matter-of-fact you can be in your manner, not embarrassed or apologetic, the less it will seem like lack of confidence to your doctor. You will have to pay for a consultation unless it is covered by your insurance policy.

I know that one important issue is how your baby's doctor feels about telephone calls. Most parents have a lot of questions about the baby in the early months. A phone call to the office is a reasonable way to get an answer to many of your questions. You may worry about whether the doctor will consider them foolish or sensible questions. It does not matter, really, except in your feelings. If you have a question, you are entitled to an answer. That is what the doctor is all about. So when looking for the right doctor for your baby, ask your friend or your obstetrician or ask directly of the doctor you are considering, what her policy is, and watch particularly the attitude shown. Is it sympathetic with the new parents' anxieties or does it reveal impatience?

A good way to come to a decision is to make an appointment with your favorite candidate and to raise your most pressing questions. It has always surprised me how few parents do this.

One matter that often gets in the way of a doctor-parent relationship is that, although the mother has made a list of her major questions, she finds that she has left it at home. Or she finds on getting home that she has forgotten to ask her major questions. Or she finds that she has forgotten some of the doctor's answers or directions. She is embarrassed to telephone so soon. No need to worry about these lapses. They happen all the time.

Many pediatricians and family doctors have a regular time of the day when they prefer telephone calls. The main problem with this is that there may be so many calls in this hour that it's irritating for the parent to run into a solid hour of busy signals. Of course, when there seems to be an emergency, the parent should call right away. In some pediatric offices, a nurse, nurse practitioner, or other member of the staff will be available for the phone calls. This is often a good system because it does not take the doctor away from seeing a patient unless the problem is more serious.

It's best to find a doctor and office staff that you are comfortable with—with their competence to care for your baby and with their openness to answer your questions.

4

The Arrival of the New Baby

Caring for a new baby is not all that different from caring for a one-, two-, or three-month old with two big exceptions. By two or three months the parents will have overcome a lot of the painful insecurity that comes from inexperience. And by three months the fretfulness and colic that so many babies show at first will have decreased a lot or disappeared.

In societies that are simpler than ours, little girls from the age of four or five years help to take care of younger brothers and sisters from early infancy. There is no such thing as inexperience, basically because there is no effective birth control so the babies keep coming. And all girls and women know how to take care of them, without anxiety—and without books. They've learned by doing, which is the natural, easy way to learn. Besides, if an unusual question comes up, there is at least one grandmother living close by to answer it right away.

I'd say the most common problem by far is trying to find the answer to the questions "Why is the baby fretting or crying, and what needs to be done?" Adults think of a wet diaper because they'd feel very uncomfortable in that situation. But if a baby (or an adult) is covered by a nightie, a sheet, and a blanket, the sensation is not coldness but warmth.

It's been a tradition of baby care that you look for an open safety pin when a baby is screaming, especially back in the days when all babies wore cloth diapers attached with pins. But in all the years that I was in practice, I never saw such an accident or heard of an actual case. It's easy to check though.

Is the crying due to hunger? That's the hardest question to answer. If you are trying to get started on breast-feeding, you want to stimulate the breasts with frequent feedings. On the other hand if you have a newborn baby who is fretful off and on, irrespective of when the last breast-feeding occurred or how much was taken, then there is no way of telling for sure whether the fretfulness, fussing, and crying means hunger or not. "Colic," which is hard crying in the late afternoon and the early evening, is much easier to diagnose because it often comes in approximately the same four-hour period each day.

When it's a question of fretfulness or hunger, you can always put the baby to breast anyway. But if the fretfulness comes very frequently, the mother may end up breast-feeding almost continually at times and that's nerve-wracking and tiring for her. One compromise is to try to avoid more than one breast-feeding per hour by substituting the pacifier, rocking in a mechanical rocker, or walking the baby. (In a bottle-fed baby you don't have to guess whether it's fretfulness or hunger. If the baby in the first month of life took at least three ounces of formula less than two hours ago, it's probably not hunger.)

In suggesting certain compromises like these I don't mean to be arbitrary; I'm only trying to keep the mother from getting exhausted. You can breast-feed almost continuously if that suits you and your baby is nursing well, seems content, and is gaining weight. If you decide to use a formula, you can offer a bottle as often as you wish. I feel that it's sensible and convenient to work gradually toward a fairly regular four-hour schedule by not being in a rush to offer a bottle just as soon as the baby stirs and whimpers. Wait a few minutes to see if she'll go back to sleep. But it you want to breast-feed, I'd advise against giving a bottle at any time in the first couple of weeks—it will discourage the breast milk production.

What is the best way to start breast-feeding and make it a success? It has been found that putting the baby to breast early, even while the mother is still in the delivery room, not only hastens bonding between them but helps both of them to make a success of breast-feeding.

Some mothers find it most comfortable to be propped up on pillows, and nurse while more or less sitting up. There can be a pillow or pillows under the baby and under the mother's arm that support the baby. The other position is with the mother lying down and facing the baby. It's helpful if a nurse specializing in breast-feeding or a member of La Leche League helps the mother find the best position.

It takes three or four days for the breast milk to come in, and many babies are designed to be somewhat sleepy and not hungry in these first few days. Then for several days they may want a dozen feedings and this stimulates the breasts to produce more and more milk. This shift is facilitated when mother and baby room-in when they are in the hospital.

One practical pattern then is to nurse the baby whenever she is fully awake and seems hungry. In traditional societies where the baby is carried almost constantly in a sling while the mother works, the baby wakes often—at even less than an hour's interval—and is put to breast promptly, soon going back to sleep, because her stomach was still partly full from the previous feeding. In our society where most babies sleep in cribs between feedings, the intervals between feedings gets longer and the amount desired gets larger.

What stimulates the breasts to produce more is how completely the breasts are emptied and how often. To give a kind-hearted bottle in the early weeks will send a signal to the breasts to diminish the supply and is to be avoided at all costs. A sensible pattern is to put the baby to breast when she wakes and cries especially if it has been two hours or more since the last feeding, one hour if you feel that she is really hungry. Let her nurse as long as she does it fairly actively on one breast. (Babies drink most of the milk in the first five minutes.) But if she still seems dissatisfied after ten or fifteen minutes, shift to the other breast for as long as she is eager. The breast to start on should be alternated at each feeding.

Some babies are slow to settle down to an efficient pattern. They nurse for a couple of minutes, then fall asleep. But when you lay them on the cool flat mattress they wake up and wail. You put them back on the breast and they promptly go to sleep again. You'll have to use your judgment. I think it's important for the inexperienced mother not to exhaust herself by trying, for an hour, to try to get the baby to nurse well. Try to limit the attempts to twice in a half hour. If unsuccessful, try to soothe the baby to sleep with a pacifier or by rocking her gently in your arms or in a mechanical rocker or in a baby carriage or by walking her or by rubbing her back. She's more likely to wake refreshed and hungry in an hour or so.

If you have decided definitely not to breast-feed, your doctor or the hospital will give you instructions for bottle-feeding of a prepared commercial formula. Infant formulas are available in three forms—powder, concentrated, and ready-to-feed. The powder and concentrated formulas require adding water; follow the directions on the can. The ready-to-feed is the most expensive form, powder the least expensive. In most communities in the United States, boiling water that's used to make formula is no longer necessary; check with your baby's doctor. Bottles, nipples, and nipple rings should be scrubbed clean with soap and water right after each use.

TIPS ON FEEDING YOUR BABY

•Formula mixing: *Powder*—one scoop powder for every two ounces water

Concentrate—equal amount of water and concentrate (for example, one can of concentrate to one can water)

Ready-to-feed—DO NOT add water

•Don't offer formula that has been out of the refrigerator more than one hour.

•If you use a pump to express your breast milk for later use, put it in a fresh plastic bag that closes with a twisty. It remains fresh for twenty-four hours in the refrigerator and for three months in the freezer.

All these directions make the care of the new baby sound complicated. But I've spent a lot of time discussing babies who have problems. But most babies don't have problems. Remember that for thousands of years mothers have successfully raised their babies with instinct and common sense and love without the help of physicians or books. You will learn fast and make a success of it.

Preparing for the New Baby

Some parents have a superstitious fear of buying any baby furniture until after the baby is born, safe and sound. The only trouble with this plan, as some new mothers have explained to me, is that if you have "baby blues" (feeling sad for a few weeks following birth)—or just feeling tired and indecisive for a few days after going home—any chore may loom large and baffling.

Let's start with a list of the things that may or may not seem essential. (Parents vary a lot in what they consider essential.)

A crib should last at least till three years of age. It should have a padded lining that goes around the inside because babies manage to squirm a lot and press their body against the sides and head of the crib. A crib's slats (the bars that form the walls of a crib) should be less than $2\frac{3}{8}$ inches apart. The mattress should fit snugly against the sides of the crib. It is usually made of foam-wrapped coiled inner springs, or foam, with a tough water-repellent covering without holes. Old-fashioned animal hair mattresses sometimes cause allergies in allergic families.

Sheets for cribs are usually made of stockinet which tucks well, stays in place, and dries quickly. Crib blankets are usually made of polyester and cotton or acrylic. It's handy to have one or two, even if you use "sleeping bags" or sleepers. You'll need a couple of waterproof sheets to protect the mattress from urine if it doesn't have its own covering.

Scales are not necessary if the baby will be visiting a doctor. They tend to get inexperienced parents over-concerned with the weight gain or lack of it.

A fabric bath with a top that turns it into a diaper-changing table is a great convenience. But a plastic tub in the kitchen sink or wash stand will do for the bathing.

Nightgowns are good for the day as well as night. The mittens are to prevent a baby from scratching her-self. Long gowns will help to keep her from kicking off the covers.

By six months, it's more practical to put her to bed in a baby sleep bag or sleeper than to try to keep her covered. The material depends on the season. Stretch suits that snap or zip from neck to foot can be used for day and night.

Disposable diapers are convenient. Diaper services are becoming less available in many communities. Some parents prefer cloth diapers and wash them at home. Two dozen will do if you wash them daily. Six dozen are ample. You'll need a large covered diaper pail.

A folding stroller, which will fit in the car, is very convenient. A government approved reclining carrier for a baby under twenty pounds may also be used as a car restraint.

A safety-tested car seat/restraint is required for all children when riding in a car—even home from the hospital following birth. Follow the directions carefully when installing the seat in your car. Babies and infants under 20 pounds are safest in a car restraint that is placed in the backseat with the baby facing the rear of the car. Many new-car dealers now offer assistance with proper use of car restraints for all babies and older children in the community.

Preparing Sibling for the New Baby

If there are older children in the family it is wise to prepare them for the new arrival as well as this can be done. That's fairly easy in the case of a child three years or older by talking about the birth of a new baby sister or brother. Some parents can't wait to announce the pregnancy as soon as it is confirmed. Other parents prefer to wait a few months to be certain that there aren't any problems with the pregnancy. You might have the child help in planning any rearrangement of the house, furniture, or clothing months ahead of time, things such as turning over the crib or part of the bureau to the baby and passing down baby clothes or baby playthings. The parents should try not to speak as if they are about to take possessions away from the child, but to offer suggestions about how the child can help and please the baby. There are many fine children's books available in a library or bookstore that help children with the arrival of a new baby.

At only two years of age, which is often the interval between first and second children, it is much more difficult to make clear to the child what will be happening and how she will feel. Letting her feel her mother's abdomen will help some, also calling attention to other babies seen in public, and asking whether the child would like to have one at home to take care of. In carrying out all these suggestions, it is wise for the parents not to act too excited or to try to get the child to be too enthusiastic. Casual is the attitude to aim for. The best you can hope for is a mixture of resentment and pleasure. If the child, before or after the baby's arrival, blurts out an aversion to having the baby at home, or suggests that he be returned to the hospital, it's wise to accept this as natural and to say, "I know how you feel; sometimes you don't want the baby at all."

It's good to realize how tactless some relatives and friends can be, including the ones who've been most enthusiastic about the older child before. I've heard a grandmother say to the older child, "This is granny's baby now!"

If the child will be going to a day-care center or nursery school, it's important that she be entered months before the baby's birth. If it's done just before or after the arrival it will seem like banishment, which accentuates the jealousy.

Preparing the Parents for the New Baby

The most important preparation for the first baby's arrival is for the prospective parents to get an idea or a feeling of what it will mean to them. In a way it is the biggest change in their lives. Until the baby's arrival they were free and independent. They could do anything, go anywhere that their work schedules allowed. But suddenly they are responsible for a second person who has many needs—frequent feedings, diaper changes, much sleep—who may cry a lot but has no words to explain what is the matter. The sense of responsibility for a wordless stranger weighs heavily on some parents especially if they are highly conscientious and the baby wakes often and fusses or cries.

The mother needs to know that she may have sad feelings ("blue spells") for a few days or even a few weeks during which she feels inexplicably pessimistic— that the baby's fretting means that he has some disease that the doctor can't diagnose or won't explain to her, that her husband doesn't love her anymore, that she has lost her attractiveness forever.

The father may be put out, consciously or unconsciously, because his wife and the baby are getting a lot of attention and he is being ignored, by relatives and friends. The feeling makes some new fathers hang around bars. Others become flirtatious with other women. Both of these reactions will naturally upset the mother even more than the blue spells or the baby's fretfulness. The couple should learn to talk about these sources of unhappiness and make very conscious efforts—not to deny their own upsetting behavior, not to argue, but to understand and make amends.

• • •

Arranging Help for Mom

There should be help for the mother for at least a couple of weeks, preferably a month, if it can be arranged. In many cases the most appropriate person is the mother's mother. They know each other's wishes and quirks. The grandmother is usually delighted to be that close to the baby from the beginning. On the other hand, there are many mothers who prefer not to call on their mothers; they are generally women who have felt belittled by their mothers all throughout childhood. They're afraid that their mothers will try to take over, and will make them feel inadequate. They may express this as an assumption that the grandmother, being of a previous generation, won't be up-to-date in her knowledge of child care.

A father may be the ideal helper especially if he can get time off from his work. Fathers should be encouraged to take time away from work and be at home during the first week following the birth of a new baby. Bonding, an emotional attachment between a baby and parent, occurs with fathers as well as mothers. Some fathers have a knack for finding out quickly and easily how to be helpful. But others are slow to catch on. There may be another relative who's willing and able to pitch in.

The alternative is to hire a woman who makes a profession of being a temporary baby nurse. Some of these are ideal: friendly, helpful, flexible. Others are opinionated, rigid, and overbearing. You should be able to get a good idea through a leisurely interview. If you find you have hired the rigid type, get rid of her right away. She'll spoil your first few weeks, which should be as happy as possible. If you don't have the courage to fire her, ask your husband or a friend to do it. I've seen cases where a bossy, possessive nurse reduced an inexperienced mother to tears, but also robbed her of the courage to dismiss her.

If I Have a Baby Boy, Should He Be Circumcised?

What I recommended about circumcision in early editions of *Baby and Child Care* and what I recommend now are quite different.

At the time of a circumcision, the sleeve of the skin which normally covers the head of the penis, called the foreskin, is cut off for religious reasons or for "cleanliness." It has been a religious tradition carried out a few days after birth for thousands of years for both Jews and Muslims, on the basis originally that God had made a covenant to this effect with Abraham. In infancy, it has usually been performed without anesthesia on the unproved assumption that babies will not remember the pain later, though they certainly cry out with pain at the time.

Back in the 1930s and 1940s, I saw several small boys who had become tense, anxious, and overprotective of their penises following circumcision performed after the age of a year. Circumcision had been prescribed in these cases because these boys had been holding onto their penises a lot, which bothered their parents. A physician had suggested in each case that the area under the foreskin may have become mildly infected, which caused itching, and that the best treatment would be to cut off the foreskin which was harboring infection.

Another factor was a parental warning that masturbation would harm the penis, a common threat in previous times. A boy might react to this fear unconsciously by holding onto his penis to protect it or to reassure himself that it was still there. In pediatric practice, I heard a number of stories from mothers confirming the frequency of this misunderstanding and how it can cause a boy to hold onto his penis. So I was able to understand why little boys become deeply upset when they are circumcised after infancy. Though the body of the penis remains, the circumcision suggests to the child that an attempt had been made to cut it off and has partially succeeded. I was convinced that circumcision after early infancy could be traumatic in the extreme and might contribute to sexual problems later in life.

When I wrote the first edition of *Baby and Child Care*, ten years after starting practice, I explained that there are three possible ways of dealing with the foreskin. I favored circumcision within a few days of birth because there would be no chance of a physician recommending the operation later in childhood and scaring the bejeebers out of a little boy. I also leaned toward circumcision right after birth because of the universal belief in medical circles at that time that women married to uncircumcised men are more likely to develop cancer of the cervix.

I also mentioned in early editions the method of daily retraction or pulling back of the foreskin, in the bath, to expose the head of the penis. Then the smegma, the waxy white material produced by the skin of the head of the penis, could be wiped off with the washcloth.

The purpose of the smegma is to lubricate the head of the penis for intercourse later, in adulthood, and to keep the foreskin from forming permanent adhesions to the head of the penis. This method appealed to some parents who disliked the idea of circumcision but wanted to go along with the prevalent notion that it was important to clean away the smegma each day. But I pointed out that there are several serious disadvantages to daily retraction. The foreskin has only a small opening in the early years. The opening relaxes and enlarges later in childhood and adolescence, so that it easily retracts during erections. Because of the small opening, retracting the foreskin forcibly over the head of the penis causes a split in the skin during the first few weeks, which is painful to the baby, makes him cry, and distresses the parents. And adhesions tend to form, which may eventually make the foreskin stick to most of the area of the head of the penis.

The other alternative, I wrote, is to leave the foreskin alone.

By the 1970s, medical opinion had swung away from the belief that it was lack of circumcision in their husbands that caused cancer of the cervix in certain groups of women. Also, by the 1970s, most physicians knew of the psychological harm from circumcision after the newborn period, and would not suggest it as a cure for holding the penis.

The American Academy of Pediatrics came to the conclusion that there is no good medical reason to recommend routine circumcision. I made the same recommendation in the 1976 revision of *Baby and Child Care*. I came out more emphatically against retraction, as ineffective, potentially distorting to the penis, and distressing to parent and baby. I advised leaving the foreskin alone.

I hoped that the controversy was settled. But in recent years it has been revived. Today there are some medical supporters of routine circumcision who believe that it will decrease, at least to a small degree, the risk of venereal diseases in adulthood such as herpes, genital warts, monillia infections, syphilis, gonorrhea, chancroid, and perhaps AIDS. But many other physicians are unconvinced, including myself.

It is true that recent studies have shown that urinary infections in infancy are less frequent in circumcised boys. But urine infection is an uncommon disease in boys (about 1 percent of boys in the first year of life). And there is no doubt that cancer of the penis is prevented by circumcision; but this is a very rare disease, causing only 150 deaths a year in the United States. Should you circumcise the two million baby boys, who are born in the United States each year, to prevent those 150 deaths later in life? Different parents may answer differently.

The American Academy of Pediatrics once again

reviewed the evidence and concluded that there may be a small benefit to circumcision after birth, but the benefit is not great enough to recommend the procedure for all newborn boys. For those parents who choose circumcision for their newborn son, pediatricians support the use of a local anesthetic so that the baby does not feel pain. I agree with this humane policy.

Parents today do have a few facts and various opinions to base their own decision on. In earliest days, parents had no idea what the issues were. The obstetrician, pediatrician, or family physician would appear at the mother's bedside a few days after delivery and say "Do you want the boy circumcised?" or "I suppose you want him circumcised." The mother, perhaps having had no conversation with her husband about this question, sometimes assented because circumcision was often presented as if it were the only sensible choice.

It may give you perspective to realize that at the end of the last century, only 5 percent of American males were circumcised, but 90 percent were circumcised by the 1960s. The percentage has decreased somewhat since then in parts of the United States. The percentage is much less in Canada, Australia, and Europe. The percentage in Britain dropped to 1 percent after the National Health Service stopped paying for routine circumcision.

My own preference, if I had the good fortune to have another son, would be to leave his little penis alone.

—5—

How Much Regularity to Infant Feeding?

In the past half century we've shifted away from extreme regularity, even rigidity, in infant feeding—exact four hour schedules: 2, 6, 10 A.M., 2, 6, 10 P.M., not ten minutes early, not ten minutes late! A prescribed amount in each bottle was essential, for instance, 3 $\frac{1}{2}$ ounces in the early weeks, not more, not less, until the doctor was consulted again. Breast-feeding was rare and unpopular in the United States before midcentury. The formula required the same proportions of milk, water, and corn syrup until the doctor decided to enlarge it or strengthen it. A new food—e.g., juice, cereal, fruit, or vegetable—was to be increased by a teaspoonful a day up to a certain limit, whether the baby was enthusiastic or reluctant.

This rigidity sounds crazy today. The reason for it was not obsessiveness or bossiness in pediatricians. It was the fear of severe diarrhea, which killed thousands of babies each summer. It was assumed that irregular schedules, irregular amounts per feeding, and carelessly made formulas were at least partly to blame. So doctors were anxious and authoritative and they put the fear of God into mothers.

By the early 1940s, pediatricians were finally convinced that bacterial contamination of cow's milk, bacterial contamination in making the formula, and inadequate refrigeration (poor families had only the window sill) were the true causes of severe diarrhea disease, not irregularity in schedules or in amounts per feeding.

Another factor in the early forties that ended the fear of irregularity was the simple but bold experiment of Frances Simsarian, a mother and a psychologist, and her pediatrician, Preston McClendon. They decided to feed Mrs. Simsarian's new baby with breast milk whenever the baby seemed hungry. They coined the phrase "self-demand feeding schedule." The baby woke little the first couple of days; then he woke, cried, and was fed ten to twelve times per twenty-four hours, at irregular intervals, for a few days. Then the baby gradually decreased the frequency of feedings down to six or seven each day. It seemed a very daring experiment at the time, and caused a lot of excitement and incredulity in pediatric circles. It had been believed previously that a baby fed whenever he cried would greedily cry more and more often, despite the fact, that's so obvious to us now, that babies had been fed "on demand" since the beginning of human development a million years ago. As a matter of fact, feeding babies mother's milk on demand is the practice in the less industrialized, developing parts of the world today.

Anyway, pediatric advice went from extreme rigidity to extreme flexibility in a very short time. When I was writing the first manuscript of *Baby and Child Care* (1943–1946), I expressed concern that some new parents might be confused to have to jump from the tradition of rigidity, that they'd heard about for years, to a new, opposite system of "self demand." I suggested that parents start with a tendency to flexibility while the baby learned about his appetite, his hunger rhythms, learned that night is for sleeping, and learned to put longer intervals between feedings. But then, as the baby showed he was ready, they could work toward greater and greater regularity.

The industrial world we live in goes by the clock, I wrote. Families must operate by the clock to one degree or another. So a baby might as well become gradually accustomed to regularity as soon as it can be done kindly, without any misery—for the baby or for the parents—whether at one month or at three months.

I also suggested working toward regularity for the benefit of those parents who had gained the impression that irregularity forever is somehow better for the child or shows that the parents are kinder or more up-to-date. To put this the other way around, I believe that it is a better philosophy, a better attitude for parents, to feel that adjusting the child to the world is one aspect of parental love, as long as it can be done without distress.

To put it more broadly, I think it is better for a child

to grow up to adulthood feeling that the greatest satisfaction in life is to serve others (rather than only to receive or to gain advantages). The way to begin adapting to the world in early infancy is gradually to accommodate to the family's hours. Of course the baby will not be aware of this point of view at first, but it will become a basic part of the parents' conscious and unconscious attitudes. And it will be gradually absorbed by the baby as he becomes increasingly aware of his parents' feelings toward him and of their expectations of him.

Do I mean that, as the baby is becoming adapted to regularity, the parents dare not give a feeding half an hour early if the baby becomes unmistakably hungry ahead of schedule, or if it suits the parents' convenience when they have a conflicting engagement? That would be taking regularity too seriously, becoming a slave to it, as in the earlier part of this century. Occasional irregularity will not disrupt the whole campaign. Even if the baby gets into a hungrier phase and clearly wants to be fed earlier at certain times of day, every day, or even seems to slip back from approximately a four-hour interval to approximately a three-hour interval all day long, my inclination would be to call that the regular schedule for the time being. You can be confident that as the baby grows older, she will always get hungry at longer and longer intervals, and find a pattern of eating about three meals a day.

But just because a baby wakes earlier than his regular pattern doesn't mean that he must be fed right away. He may be happy to watch his mobile or his mother or father for a half hour or so. The tendency to greater wakefulness, especially in the afternoon, is progressive throughout infancy just as is the tendency to longer intervals between hunger needs. So wait and see if your baby will be content to wait until nearly his accustomed feeding time.

A problem that often puzzles parents, whether they are inclined toward a demand schedule or are working toward regularity, is to know whether the baby's crying means hunger or whether it is due to some other discomfort such as "three-month colic" (a daily period of severe abdominal cramps lasting three or four hours, with abdominal distention and the noisy passing of gas, most commonly in the late afternoon and early evening); or "fretfulness" which is not as severe as colic but can occur at any time of day.

A rough rule to help you decide is that, if the baby has slept for two or more hours after a feeding, consider it hunger and offer another feeding. But if the crying begins soon after a satisfactory feeding (steady nursing for twenty minutes or the emptying of a bottle), it's probably not hunger. Try a pacifier or walking the baby for twenty minutes, before trying another feeding.

Whether you incline to regularity or flexibility in a feeding schedule, it's good to know that breast-fed babies commonly want to be fed again two or three hours after the last feeding, but babies on the bottle often learn to last about three and one-half or four hours between feedings.

A pleasant advantage of having accustomed a baby

to a fairly regular feeding schedule is that he's not accustomed to being fed immediately after waking. As a result, he may be willing, if he wakes about 6 A.M., to wait up to another hour for his first morning feeding, perhaps babbling, perhaps going back for another snooze. So his regularity may provide an irregularity that's to your benefit. But if you are to enjoy this benefit you must accustom yourself not to run into his room at his first stirring in the morning.

So far I haven't emphasized the differences between breast- and bottle-feeding. Certainly breast-feeding introduces another very crucial factor into the issue of how much regularity is desirable or practical in infant feeding schedules. The breasts have a marvelous system for adapting to the appetite of the baby—the more he wants, the longer he nurses, and the more completely he empties the breasts. This early and complete emptying of the breasts is what stimulates them to produce more milk. The opposite effect is that the less often the nursing, the less often the complete emptying of the breasts, a message will be sent to the milk-secreting glands to cut down on the amount of milk produced. This is why complementing several breast-feedings each day with some formula is so depressing to success at breast-feeding—especially when starting to breast-feed in the newborn period.

So, in one sense, trying to work toward regularity in a feeding schedule is potentially inhibiting to success at breast-feeding particularly in the first few weeks, before the breast milk supply has been well established. I think the answer, in the first month or two of breast-feeding, is to give priority to stimulating the breasts by letting the baby nurse as often and as irregularly and as long as he wishes, within reason. Then, when he is getting enough to regularly keep him content for two or two and one-half or three hours, you can begin to work toward regularity by waking him after he has slept for three hours, and by letting him lie awake if he has waked less than three hours from the last feeding provided he is content to do so. But I wouldn't make him wait if he is crying hard from hunger.

When I said in the last paragraph "nurse as often and as irregularly and as long as he wishes, within reason," I was thinking of the mother who is particularly eager to nurse and the difficult baby who wakes very often, is put to breast, but goes right back to sleep again after only a couple of minutes of irregular nursing. When he is put back in his crib, though, he wakes promptly or after a few minutes and starts crying again. This situation is intensely frustrating and exhausting for the mother, as well as it must be for the baby. It seems to the mother as if she is trying to nurse all day long and half the night. She gets little rest, and worries constantly. I think that she should not feel obliged to keep nursing so much of the time. It is obviously not adequately emptying or stimulating the breasts. She might give the baby two chances to nurse within an hour, and allow him a limit of fifteen minutes for each feeding. Then she might put him to bed with a pacifier for an hour or two, if he only fusses. If he cries hard, she can carry him or rock him in his carriage for twenty minutes. Or if the father or a friend is available, he can give the baby an automobile ride, to allow the mother a more complete rest.

It's well to remember that the mother's fatigue and tension, from the baby's behavior at the breast, may be interfering with her "let down reflex" which is meant to release and gently expel the milk, in response to his hunger crying or nursing. So it's a vicious circle. That's why I'm suggesting that she set limits to the nursing time, to give herself a rest from the effort and strain. Better still is if she can soothe herself by getting her mind on something else altogether, whether it's television, music, reading, or asking a friend to visit. If nothing works at all, she can experiment with giving a bottle of formula. If the baby swallows it all down and goes contentedly to sleep for three or four hours, it suggests that the strain has been interfering seriously with the let-down reflex and that weaning to the bottle should be considered, at least for a day or two. Meanwhile the mother's milk can be pumped or expressed.

One of the unfortunate results of the combination of bottle-feeding and the rigid feeding philosophy of the past was that parents became accustomed to the idea that babies will expect to (and should) consume exactly the same amount of formula at each feeding. After all, the parents could see how much if any was left in the bottle and would feel it was their duty to nudge the baby to finish. This urging sometimes led to feeding problems. When studies were made of how many ounces different babies took from the breast at different feedings, by weighing them before and after, it was found that wide variations were the rule. At 6 A.M., when the mother's breasts may have had a long time to rest during the evening, a baby might take as much as ten ounces, but be quite satisfied with three ounces at 6 P.M. when mother and baby might be tired.

I'll try to summarize and simplify a complex issue. I prefer the philosophy of working gradually toward regularity, after the age of a month or two, by waking the breast-fed baby after three hours (if he'll wake), the bottle-fed baby after four hours. If a breast-fed baby wakes two hours after the last feeding (or a bottle-fed baby three hours after the last feeding), I'd encourage him to wait up to an hour, with a pacifier, provided he's content or fusses only occasionally. Or see if walking him for ten minutes will send him back to sleep again. But if he cries hard or fusses steadily you should feed him.

I prefer working gently toward regularity in a moderate way, especially for the inexperienced parents' convenience. They have needs too, and they don't have to be slaves to the baby in order to be kind. If this balance between considerations for the baby and consideration for parents gets established early, the baby will gradually come to feel comfortable with this feeding pattern. He will be less likely to be demanding and tempestuous in his second year and after, more inclined to be cooperative and polite. And the parents, not having sacrificed too much, will not be so ready to get mad when he disappoints them.

But if my advice doesn't appeal to you, if you think I'm overemphasizing the value of regularity, if you incline to a demand schedule, you've got lots of company and I understand that point of view. It's your baby. Parents must follow their own convictions; other people's convictions won't work for them.

When a Mother Thinks About Going Back to Work

When is a good time for mothers who've held outside jobs (either of necessity or choice) to plan to go back to work? The longer they can have to feel they are mothers the better; of course, it will depend on family finances. Breast-feeding can often be continued after returning to work by bringing the baby to the office, or by one trip home if it's not too far, both of which will depend on the tolerance of the boss and of fellow workers. Or someone can feed the baby a bottle. (However, the fewer the bottles the longer the breast-feeding can be maintained.)

Whether the mother takes full care for one, three, six, nine, or twelve months, the shift to the substitute child care person should be gradual so that the baby will feel familiar and secure with the substitute before the mother begins absenting herself. Though it may seem like an extravagance, it is vitally important, from

my point of view and from the baby's point of view. I'd
say that two weeks of overlapping care should be the
minimum, better three or four weeks.

Some mothers get easily tired in the newborn
period and may need protection from too many visitors
and visitors who stay too long. (I recall, from several
hospitalizations as an adult, how trapped I felt by some
visitors. Of course, I was brought up to be very polite
and couldn't say, "I'm tired. Will you please leave." And
there was not a way I could jump out of bed and
depart!) If a mother finds she gets tired with visitors
she can say to friends who call ahead, "My doctor
doesn't want me to have more than two visitors a day,
for the time being." Or, "He doesn't want visits to last
more than five minutes for now." If the visitor hasn't
called ahead and is a bore, you can pretend to go to
sleep right in the middle of the conversation!

—6—

Beginning Solids

A baby's first solid food is a big event—not only for the baby but also for the parents. It seems, at the time, as significant a forward step as graduation from high school or even college.

My mother told me that when I was a baby ninety years ago, we babies didn't get any solids until one year of age. That rule, like others, was established by Dr. Emmett Holt's book, *The Care and Feeding of Children,* which my mother followed religiously, at least with her first child or two. I didn't think of being the first as an advantage. When I got into a quarrel with a younger sibling my mother always put the blame on me, saying, "Benny, you should have known better; you are the oldest." And she was always stricter in applying the rules with me, it seemed to me. For example, I wasn't allowed to eat even half a banana until I was twelve years old, because Dr. Holt said they were too indigestible. But I remember that rule being relaxed progressively with each of my subsequent sisters and brother.

When I started pediatric practice in New York City in 1933, the most usual age for starting first solids was five months. When *Baby and Child Care* was published in 1946 the most common age was three months.

A few years later, some physicians suggested starting cereal at one month and adding vegetables, fruit, and beef by three months. Why the rush? Beginning mothers were eager to have their babies keep up with—or even excel—their relative's or neighbor's babies. Some doctors were eager to compete with others, in being "advanced."

Then gradually it was realized that much of the very early solids were not being digested, and that they sometimes interfered with the success of breast-feeding, which was beginning to be popular. So now we are back to five or six months as the time to begin solid food. I am strongly in favor of delaying solids until five or six months.

Cereal has generally remained the traditional first solid food, probably because it is bland and it rarely causes indigestion or allergy (except in the occasional case of a wheat allergy). The commercial rice cereal made for babies is fortified with iron, a necessary nutrient after six months of life for nursing babies and those not getting enough iron in formula.

I deviated from tradition in my practice and suggested apple sauce or raw, ripe banana as a first solid, because some babies are unenthusiastic about cereal for a while, and I was very reluctant to get them prejudiced or antagonistic toward any food.

Speaking of lack of enthusiasm for solids reminds me of how puzzled babies behave toward any first solid. They wrinkle up their noses. They block the food with their tongues, they push it around, and they make clacking noises. All of this pushes most of the food out of the mouth and onto the chin. The mother shaves as much as she can with the spoon and tries to get it back into the mouth by scooping it off the spoon against the upper lip. Most of it oozes out again onto the chin but a little gets swallowed on each try.

It's not surprising that this skill takes time to learn. The spoon is a strange object! The muscles of the mouth are accustomed to squeezing milk between the nipple and the roof of the mouth and then it is pushed down the throat. The baby must learn to catch the food with the tip of the tongue, move it back over the top of the tongue and start it down the throat with a "milking" motion of the tongue and throat. Fortunately, for most babies this remarkably complex set of movements takes only a few days or weeks to learn.

Which Solids, in What Order?

Up to a few years ago, almost all doctors recommended starting with cooked cereal, then adding strained, boiled, or steamed vegetables, strained stewed fruit, scraped beef, and hard-boiled egg white. Egg yolk is postponed to the last quarter of the first year because it may cause allergy in some children. Later introduction of other foods also lessens the chance of allergies in susceptible families. Chicken and white fish such as sole, haddock, and halibut are commonly introduced early in the second year.

Baby foods in cans or jars are convenient to store and to warm up, and can be as nutritious as fresh cooked foods. But some manufacturers mix the fruit, vegetables, and meats with cereals. I think it is wiser to buy such foods separately so that you will know what you are serving and you will know if vegetables, fruits, and meats are diluted with cereals. For if a baby is getting plain cereals or puddings from some jars, cereals mixed with vegetables, fruits, and meats from others, the diet may be lopsidedly starchy. Read the fine print to learn what your baby is eating.

It is wise not to add salt to a baby's or child's foods. The desire for salt can easily become a lifelong habit that favors high blood pressure, heart disease, and stroke.

It is often convenient to give the baby the same cooked vegetables and fruits, fresh or canned, that the rest of the family are eating. These foods should be strained so that prior to one year your baby can swallow the food with comfort and safety. You can shift gradually to lumpy vegetables and fruits after a year, whether fresh or canned or in "junior food" jars. Canned fruit for adults is often full of syrup which is not advisable and should be poured off.

In recent years there have been small but increasing numbers of nutritionists and physicians (including myself) who recommend a vegetarian diet with not only no meat, chicken, or fish, but no animal fats, no dairy (cream, butter, cow's milk, or cheese), and little vegetable fat. Their reasoning has been as follows:

- Food preferences are usually formed in early childhood and then tend to persist.

- Americans are eating ever more fatty diets and the proportion of obese children and adults keeps increasing.

- Deaths from coronary artery arteriosclerosis (heart attack), from certain cancers and from stroke keep increasing. They have been linked to high fat diets, particularly animal fat (meat, chicken, fish, eggs, dairy products).

- A major reason parents do not heed the danger of high fat diets to their children seems to be because the deaths do not occur until middle age.

I advise withholding cow's milk ("pasteurized milk" and prepared formula) until after the age of two or three years. I also recommend withholding meat, chicken, fish, eggs, cheese not only in infancy but at any age. I have been on such a diet for several years, with good results. This is not a reason for others to do the same, but it shows I'll take my own medicines.

But there are still many nutritionists and physicians who are doubtful whether a child over the age of two years on a vegetarian diet (without meats, chicken, cheese, eggs, and particularly milk, which is in a special category that I'll discuss next) can get enough calories, calcium, and high quality protein to thrive. I am not a researcher or expert on this question; but I have been convinced by nutritionists and physicians who have studied it carefully and at length. They believe that a variety of vegetables, fruits, whole grains, and beans will cover all of a young child's needs *after the age of two years.*

Up to the age of two years, I am strongly in favor of breast-feeding if the mother is willing and able. Second best is the prepared formula, liquid or powdered, based on cow's milk. The proportions of protein and fat in the formulas have been reduced and the sugar has been increased to make it closer to human milk in composition.

Breast milk confers partial immunity to some intestinal and respiratory infections. It is less likely to cause allergy and perhaps less likely to favor diabetes. Babies who breast-feed have fewer ear infections than those who take formula. However, if a mother chooses not to breast-feed or is unable to breast-feed (because of insufficient milk—this is rare—or a medical reason), prepared formula is better than pasteurized or evaporated milk formulas made at home.

The idea of eliminating cow's milk after the age of two or three years, and not introducing such dairy products as cheese and yogurt, is shocking to many people who have been accustomed to hearing it advertised as the best all-around food for children and recommended in amounts from a pint to a quart a day. In my childhood the milkman delivered six quarts for six children!

It's important to realize that for most of the world's children, the feeding of milk does not go beyond weaning from the mother's breast, typically at two years.

The Physician's Committee for Responsible Medicine concluded that children can get sufficient calories, calcium, and high grade protein from a diet of vegetables, whole grains, and beans. Animal feeding experiments that have looked at various diets show that extra rapid growth and development from extra rich diets may be thought of as atypical and *may* lead to death from "old age" earlier than the average. The children who are given a diet without meats and dairy products may avoid arteriosclerotic heart disease, certain cancers, and stroke when on such a diet for life. More information about preparing this type of diet for young children is available in *Baby and Child Care* (7th edition).

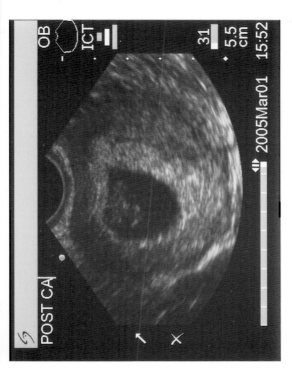

7

Poor Eaters

There were many, many children all over America who had feeding problems in the 1930s, when I started pediatric practice. This was primarily because with new knowledge about nutrition but with only meager understanding about children's emotional development, doctors where taught in medical school that it was their responsibility to impress mothers with the need for a carefully balanced diet, sufficient calories and vitamins, on a rigid and regular schedule. So conscientious physicians put the fear of God into conscientious parents, and children's stomachs rebelled.

Today when physicians recommend flexibility with choice of food and amounts at each meal, there are many fewer eating problems but there are still some. A few cases of poor eating in childhood are due to chronic illness; but in most of these cases, the appetite was good up to a point but then turned poor. In a child with a chronic disease, there are other symptoms of illness.

Children all have different patterns of development. Some are born to be tall, others short. Some are heavy-boned, others slender-boned. Some are muscular others not. Some put on weight with the greatest of ease even though they appear to be eating lightly; others eat huge meals and remain skinny. It's very hard for some parents to accept these individual differences. They have a picture of the ideal boy or girl in mind and can't help but consider any other shape as unfortunate and needing correction. These parents may be unhappy if a daughter is big-boned and overly robust or if a son is short or delicately structured.

A moderate number of fair eaters are eating and growing well enough according to their genetic patterns, which considers the growth of their parents and other members of the family. Their low normal weight levels and small appetites have been that way since birth, so they aren't the result of pushing or forcing. They aren't really having eating problems except that their parents would like them to be huskier in build and heartier in appetite. But the parents are too wise to be urging all the time, realizing that this would only lower the appetite further.

It's important to make this point about parents who are unhappy about their children's genetically determined shapes because the more they urge slender children with naturally small appetites to eat a little more, the more they depress their children's appetites. Or if they try to hold back on the intake of a plump child, they may increase her craving for food and they may tempt her to cheat between meals.

The great majority of children who are poor eaters don't start that way but are made that way because at some period of their development their parents became anxious and tried to push or force them to eat more than they wanted.

I remember, way back in my own childhood, when I was lying in bed with a fever and smelled the lunch cooking in the kitchen and how disgusted I felt that anyone could eat something that smelled so bad. Often it takes a number of days after an illness for the appetite to return. A parent who has been concerned about the total lack of appetite during the feverish stage finds it particularly difficult to refrain from urging a child to eat as soon as the fever subsides. Yet this is a crucial period, for a temporary loss of appetite during sickness can be turned into a permanent poor appetite in just a few days if food is pushed during this period of aversion.

If you can wait a few more days, you'll be rewarded by a better-than-ever appetite when the body has rid itself of the infection. I remember a few occasions when the appetite eventually rebounded with such vigor that the mother called me to ask if any harm could result when a child not only ate huge meals but sometimes begged for more an hour after a meal was done. So patience and trust in nature are the treatment and the way to the prevention of feeding problems after illness.

There are other typically critical times when problems begin. One, as you can imagine, is when a premature baby is finally brought home from the hospital after weeks of worry. He weighs enough that the doctors consider him out of danger, but he may still look like a starving creature to the parents. It's very hard for them to avoid worrying and pushing as much milk as they can get into the small baby. Since the temptation is so great, so is the need for the parents to train themselves from the start to stop the feeding at breast or bottle just as soon as the baby loses interest. Don't try to "get in just a little more." You may succeed, but at the cost of reducing the appetite for the next feeding and the next and the next. It's a losing game.

Some eating problems begin with the introduction of solid food, if the doctor seems to imply, or if the parent gets the impression elsewhere, that the baby will be eager to gobble up more each day. Actually, it takes babies a number of days to get used to the first solid foods: the hard spoon, the sticky consistency, the need to work the food from the front of the mouth to the rear where the swallowing mechanism can get hold of it. The whole business is so strange that most babies have a facial expression that looks more like disgust than eagerness! They leave their tongues in the front of their mouths as they work their jaws up and down, so that nine-tenths of the food is pushed right back out of the mouth onto the chin. But after four or five times, most of the teaspoonful has been swallowed.

Don't attempt to get more than a teaspoonful in until the baby has learned the trick and is showing a little eagerness. This may easily take a week or two. I've often heard parents say, "If I try once more, I often get one more teaspoonful in." It seems like a gain at that meal, but over the weeks and months it works against appetite. Stop spooning any food just as soon as you see the slightest sign of lack of enthusiasm, not when the child finally turns his head away or clamps his jaw shut. That's the way you keep his appetite high.

Cereal is the traditional first solid food, but stewed or pureed fruit in jars, such as applesauce or raw ripe mashed banana, arouses enthusiasm sooner, so I think it's a preferable first solid. Since babies have been on just milk up to this time, many of them are frantic for breast or bottle when hungry and are frustrated when offered the unmanageable teaspoon of solid food first. If so, give the breast or bottle first. Later, after the baby has learned that solids satisfy hunger too, you can give the solids first.

Occasionally a baby seems to lose some of its appetite around six months of age. This is a time when the monthly weight gain, which may have been averaging one and one-half pounds, is apt to drop down to a pound or less per month, with a corresponding drop in eagerness for food. It's also a time when a baby develops new skills that stimulate a greater interest in other things around her. Sitting up without support lets her experience her parents and other things from a different view than when she was on her back. Reaching out and grasping an attractive toy with recently developed hand skills and back-and-forth baby talk are other activities that may distract some babies from a major interest in food.

The most common time for the start of a feeding problem is between twelve and fifteen months. For reasons that I don't fully understand, a majority of babies turn against some foods that they took willingly enough before. One factor may be that their weight gaining now declines to half a pound per month. Another factor may be the baby's increasing sense of their individuality and their impulse to make their own decisions about the foods they prefer. Most frequently rejected is some or all of the vegetables. Why these aversions to formerly accepted foods? Perhaps we will know some day. Some of them last only a few days, other for months, others for life. Many adults too experience shifts in appetite. Is it that infants' bodies have enough of some ingredients for the time being? Is it because body growth continues to slow down, until the puberty growth spurt? In any case we need to respect these variations because we only make matters worse by trying to interfere.

You don't need to worry or insist that the baby eat an undesired food. Serve the food that the baby still enjoys. Try a new vegetable that is easy to swallow. If all vegetables are turned down, remember that fruits and milk will cover the same nutritional needs as vegetables did. Your doctor may suggest a daily multivitamin during this brief period when certain foods are rejected by your baby.

A second food that is often rejected at this time is cereal, particularly for supper. You can branch out into other oat and whole wheat cereals—cooked or "dry." You can offer breads, toast, plain unsweetened crackers made from whole wheat, rye, or oats. These are just as valuable as cereals.

A third food whose intake is often reduced at about a year of age is milk. This is particularly apt to alarm parents because milk has the reputation of being the cornerstone of nutrition at this age. But if a small child continues to take a pint of milk a day on the average, this should cover the needs for calcium and good protein. If the average intake of milk continues to fall below a pint, you can make the cereal with milk, mix soup with milk, offer small pieces of cheese. An ounce of firm cheese contains as much calcium as 8 ounces of milk. If all of these milk substitutes are rejected, the doctor can prescribe a calcium supplement.

Fruits continue to retain their popularity in a great majority of children. During the second year of life, vegetables, cereal, and milk usually regain their appeal, provided the parents haven't made an issue of them.

In preventing or treating feeding problems in the one-year-old, it is crucial that the child be feeding herself, which children can do by fifteen months if encouraged. I've heard parents say, "She can eat the fruit by herself but I have to feed her the vegetables." No! No! If she's capable of feeding herself one, she's capable of feeding herself the other. To go on feeding her the vegetables keeps reminding her that she doesn't really like them and increases her aversion. Give her more opportunities to lead the way and to learn to enjoy feeding all foods to herself.

Let the one-year-old learn to use a spoon as soon as he shows the ambition. The sooner he takes over the feeding the less temptation you'll have to urge. You'll have to put up with the mess. For if you wait to let him hold his own spoon until he's skillful, he may have lost that particular ambition and just wait for you to feed him. While he's learning the use of the spoon, you can be using your spoon to feed him at the same time.

The treatment of poor eating is simple enough to prescribe but very difficult for most parents to carry out. It is to offer the baby or child only those foods which are appealing at the present. There is no need to urge or bribe or threaten . . . or scold. I mean this literally even if, as I've seen in a couple of families, the child was down to peanut butter on saltine crackers. Is this a good diet? No, but it will ward off starvation. And I don't know any other way to work at it. After the child has been on a diet which he enjoys for a month or two you can try, very casually, to introduce a food he used to like. Whether or not he eats any of it, try another once-liked food in another month. Don't be in a hurry. Don't scold or argue or make an issue. Be friendly. Eating is meant to be a pleasant ceremony, not a battle.

My main point is, what is the alternative? I know that you can't force a child to eat what she dislikes. So all you can do, aside from providing substitutes that the child still likes, is to accustom her to think of mealtimes as pleasurable again and hope that over a period of months and years she'll forget some of her aversions and try these foods again. I know it can happen if the parents are able to discipline themselves not to offer rejected foods again for at least six months and not to force a food that the child dislikes. Serve small portions, to encourage the child to have to ask for more instead of the large helpings you'd like her to eat but which make her say—or feel—"I can't eat all that!" As a teenager, I eventually got to love squash that nauseated me at four years of age.

Will a lopsided diet lead to disease, either a nutritional deficiency disease or infection due to lowered resistance? I have dealt with dozens and dozens of feeding problems, some of them quite severe, but I've been surprised that none of them have shown evidence of either type of disease. One possible and likely explanation is that the published standards for what are considered ideal intakes of all the elements in a proper diet are set at very generous levels, to be on the safe side. To express this the other way around, when a dietary element is in short supply the body can make do with considerably less than an ample supply.

You can see that the prevention and cure of feeding problems, at whatever stage of development, is really the same:

- Let the baby or child think of food as something she wants, not as something which is pushed at her.

- Don't try to get in one speck more after she has shown she is satisfied.

- Don't make her turn her head away. Always try to stop before that point is reached.

- Every baby is born with at least a reasonably good appetite. Think of it as a precious possession to be preserved at all costs.

8

Common Physical Problems

Teething

There used to be a lot of folklore about teething: that it often brought fever (at times, a high fever), ear infections, vomiting, diarrhea, and convulsions. A reaction set in in scientific pediatric centers denying these dramatic consequences, because more accurate means of diagnosis and research showed that there were other causes of such symptoms. I think that the reaction went a little too far. I feel—though I have no proof—that some colds and stomach and intestinal disturbances in infants and young children are helped to get started by a lowered resistance during the most active stages of teething. Of course this is the age when colds and their complications are most common and often last longest. And it's also the age when all the baby teeth erupt, often producing such symptoms as excessive drooling, a craving to bite anything bitable, fretfulness, for as long as three months with each set of teeth.

I say some colds and intestinal disturbances are helped to get going by very active teething because there are great differences between individuals in this regard. At one extreme are the unfortunate babies and small children who are miserable—and make the whole family miserable—whenever they are teething. And you have to remember that the teeth tend to erupt in separate groups, each group taking about three months to erupt; so that adds up to fifteen months out of the first thirty months of life for teething symptoms in those who do show symptoms—half of the first two and one-half years of life. It's no wonder that these babies seem always to be teething and snuffling.

At the other extreme are the babies who show no distress. The mother hears a clicking noise from the spoon and discovers the first tooth, to her great surprise.

The age when the first tooth appears varies greatly. On occasion, a baby is born with a tooth! At the other extreme are those healthy babies who wait until they are a year old, and give their parents the suspicion that perhaps they won't ever have any. The average age for the eruption of the first tooth is seven months, and the average age when teething symptoms first begin— chewing on chewable objects including hands and clothing, noticeable drooling, fretfulness—is three or four months. So it takes about three months of teething before each group of teeth appear.

The sequence of the eruption of the groups is usually the same: first the two lower central incisors (the cutting teeth). Next, more or less together, the two upper central incisors and the four lateral incisors (next to the central incisors) come through. On the average these eight incisors are in by about a year of age. In the first part of the second year come the four first molars. These first molars are more likely to cause discomfort and interference with sleep than the earlier groups, perhaps because they are larger. They come in far enough back to leave space for the pointed canine (dog) teeth which erupt in the second half of the second year. Between two and two and one-half years come the second molars.

There is almost never any connection between the earliness or lateness of the appearance of the teeth, and earliness or lateness of other aspects of child development such as age of walking, talking, or the eventual level of intelligence.

There are twenty baby (or primary) teeth. The crowns, the part of the teeth that will be visible, were being formed in the gums before the baby was born so their makeup depends on the mother eating a balanced diet during her pregnancy—green vegetables, fruits, whole-grain cereals and breads, and legumes (beans) two or three times a day. She can be extra reassured of her calcium, if she wishes, by drinking skim milk; but this is not essential if she is eating lots of fruits, vegetables, whole grains, and beans two or three times a day and taking a prenatal multivitamin pill.

The permanent teeth begin with the six-year-old

molars that come in farther back than the second baby molars. The permanent incisors and canines must make space for themselves by destroying the roots of the baby incisors and canines. In the same way the baby molars fall out, making room for the permanent "bicuspids" (which have only two cusps instead of the four cusps of the molars). Behind the permanent six-year molars eventually come the twelve-year-old molars and the eighteen-year-old molars. (The latter may never erupt.) The crowns of the permanent teeth are being laid down during the mother's pregnancy as well as during early childhood, and depend on good nutrition in both mother and child—whole grain cereals, leafy and root vegetables, fruits, and beans.

The main threat to the health of the teeth—baby and permanent—is decay, which starts with cavities. The cavities are dissolved in the enamel of the teeth by lactic acid that is formed out of sugar by bacteria which live in gummy "plaques" on the surface of the teeth.

The longer the teeth are bathed in sweet saliva each day and night and the more plaque on the teeth, the greater the likelihood of cavities. That is why wise parents avoid giving their children sweet snacks such as lollipops, candy, dried fruit (such as dates, apricots, and prunes), cookies, cake, sweet drinks, especially between meals.

There is a particularly rapid form of decay after any teeth have erupted which may occur when a baby is regularly put down to sleep on her back with a bottle of juice or formula. It's wise to avoid this practice. If a baby needs a bottle before sleep, I suggest that she be held by the parent so that the formula or juice does not pool around the teeth and create cavities. When juice is given to a baby, it should be diluted with water (one part juice to two or three parts water) to limit the amount of sugar that the baby takes in.

Some parents, for reasons I don't fully understand, pull the baby's hand out of his mouth every time they see him chewing his hand during teething spells. The best course when a teething baby chews his hand is to give him a hard rubber ring or other hard rubber teething object. Avoid thin, brittle plastic toys which easily break and may cause choking. Don't use any drug without the doctor's advice.

Fluoride in the proper amount has been found to be very valuable in protecting the teeth against decay. It can't do a complete job but it reduces decay by about 40 percent, which is very worthwhile. Its value was discovered in the finding that in those parts of the world where fluoride occurs naturally in the water in a concentration of about one part to a million, there is the 40 percent reduction in decay. When fluoride is added to the water supply in regions where it does not occur naturally, it has the same beneficial effect. The main problem with fluoride is that if it occurs naturally or is added to the water supply in amounts way beyond one part in a million, it may cause mottling (small pits) of the enamel. This is not harmful except that it is unsightly looking in the extreme case. Once in the enamel there is no way of getting it out.

The ideal situation is when the fluoride concentration in the water supply is naturally about one part per million. Then there is nothing to argue about. But if there is no fluoride naturally occurring in the water supply in the region and the dental, medical, and public health professionals propose adding it, there often develops a countermovement organized by people who philosophically or temperamentally are opposed to any such introduction of a foreign substance into the human body. They convince themselves and each other that such foreign substances will have a poisonous effect causing cancers, heart disease, and other ills. People with such suspicions fought vigorously against the use of vaccination to prevent small pox many years ago, and people with similar attitudes are fighting today against the obligatory use of the vaccines designed to prevent whooping cough, measles, diphtheria, and tetanus. Remember that fluoride is a normal, natural ingredient of water in many parts of our country and the world.

If natural fluoride is not in your city or well water in adequate amounts to prevent tooth decay, and it hasn't been added, your dentist can treat your family's teeth by application of fluoride or recommend a fluoridated toothpaste. Your doctor or dentist may also recommend a fluoride supplement as a tablet or liquid.

Tooth-brushing should begin as soon as there is one tooth. Use a soft brush with only water or a small amount of toothpaste since a young child will swallow the paste rather than spit out the excess. A great time to begin brushing the teeth of a small child is when she is calm and lying in your lap. A song and a smile make it a pleasant adventure.

What about dental visits? Children's dentists recommend half-yearly visits beginning when the first tooth appears. This is to examine the teeth, discuss dental care including flossing and to accustom the young child to the dentist and what the dentist does, before any problems have developed. It's well worthwhile starting early, at around the first birthday.

Sneezing, Coughing and Dripping . . . the Common Cold

Colds in the early stages are caused by viruses—small germs that can't be seen with a standard microscope. There are a number of different cold viruses, so that your baby cannot develop immunity to all viruses. Young children, (between one and four years old) have an average of seven virus infections each year. The average number of colds gradually decreases with age— four at nine years, two at twelve. It's no wonder that young children always seem to have a cold!

It used to be thought that the viruses were mainly passed by spray caused by a cough or sneeze from the nose and throat. Recent research has shifted the blame to the hands. So it's worthwhile to wash your hands frequently if you have a cold, or if you are caring for a child with a cold.

What other precautions are worthwhile to avoid

spread? Tests have shown that, when parents wear a mask that covers the nose and mouth, it is not effective in preventing spreading a cold virus. In a small house or apartment, it is not worth all the fuss and scolding to try to keep the child with a cold from mixing with the other children. It may be different with a large house in which the child with a cold can be conveniently isolated.

Certainly it's worthwhile with children of all ages to avoid any contact with children from other families who have colds, indoors or outdoors. Unfortunately this can't be accomplished if your child attends a day-care center or nursery school, or receives family day care, even if the staff are strict in excluding or isolating any child with a cold. Remember that colds are contagious for a couple of days before any symptoms appear. I do not feel that this is sufficient cause to keep a child out of group care unless there are extraordinary health risks for your child.

The virus stage of colds lasts only three to ten days, but the reason that many colds last longer is that the resistance of the tissues of the nose, throat, and bronchial tubes (or airways) is lowered by the viral infection. This makes it possible for various harmful bacteria, which are sometimes inhabitants of the nose and throat but held at bay by the body's resistance, to overcome that resistance. So it's the bacteria (the "secondary invaders") not the original virus infection that cause some colds to last more than a few days or go on to complications such as ear infections ("otitis"), sinusitis, or pneumonia.

An adult feels the beginning of a cold in a runny nose and perhaps a slightly scratchy throat. A child's cold may start with a fever. Then the nose symptoms may show up a day or two later when the fever has subsided, or there may be no fever to start with—just the runny nose. When a complication such as an ear infection or sinusitis sets in, a fever, ear pain or more frequent coughing may develop.

You can't judge the severity of a cold or its complications by the presence or absence of fever. An infant can be quite sick with the complications of a cold without any fever. On the other hand, many children by the time they are two or three years old will start some of their colds and sore throats with a high fever. They may look flushed or lose appetite but otherwise seem comfortable. When children get to be five or ten years, they are less and less likely to start with a fever. But when a fever occurs later in a cold, it is likely to point to a complication and requires a doctor's prompt examination.

In infants, you judge the seriousness of a cold, cold complication, throat infection, or other infectious disease by how sick the baby seems—listlessness, unhappiness, pallor, weak from fatigue, loss of appetite for food, in other words by how differently the baby looks or behaves compared to his usual appearance. Bronchitis and sinusitis are signaled by increased frequency of cough, ear infection by rubbing the ear, or a persistent cry of pain.

Infants snuffle with a nose cold and this can make the parents very uncomfortable in sympathy. But the babies themselves don't usually mind. An efficient way to relieve the snuffles is to use a rubber bulb nose syringe. Squeeze the bulb flat with one hand *before* inserting the tip. Then insert the tip for about an eighth to a quarter of an inch and release the bulb which will suck the mucus out. The important thing is not to blow the mucus further into the nose by compressing the bulb after the tip is inserted.

When the back of the nose gets stuffy with the mucus from a cold, it is more bothersome than bubbliness for babies. They may have such a strong inclination to keep their mouths shut, awake or asleep, that the congestion makes them angry if awake and wakes them repeatedly whenever they fall asleep.

There are several ways of treating stuffiness. The most effective, especially during the season when homes are heated, is to get extra moisture into the air. An inexpensive cool mist humidifier does an adequate job at under thirty dollars. The best and most expensive is an ultrasonic humidifier, which may cost anywhere from forty to four hundred dollars. (The reservoir of either should be cleaned weekly when in use, with a solution of a cup of chlorine bleach in a gallon of water, to prevent growth of bacteria and molds.)

An electric steam vaporizer gets moisture into the air by boiling water with an electric heating element. It's inexpensive but it heats up the room and is less safe because a small child may knock it over. Get one that turns itself off when empty and be sure to place in a safe place in the room.

Nose drops may be composed simply of a saline solution which you can buy or make yourself with one-fourth teaspoon of table salt in four ounces of water. It will thin or soften thick mucus which then can be more easily sucked out with a bulb syringe.

Medicated nose drops shrink the tissues of the inside of the nose, making more room for breathing and discharge of mucus. There are two problems with medicated nose drops. When used frequently there is apt to be a reaction to the shrinkage, in which the tissues puff up to more than normal size. So they should not be used more than once every four to six hours or continued for more than a week on the doctor's recommendation.

Another disadvantage is that a small child is apt to fight against them. Then the child gets upset and no drops get into the nose. Still they may be worth the effort if a baby is frantic with a blocked nose from the congestion—unable to breathe if he insists on closing his mouth, unable to nurse at breast or bottle. Be quick about instilling them and don't try to hold the baby's head—he hates that. The baby's doctor or nurse practitioner will recommend the type and amount of nose drops.

Older, cooperative children can be on their backs across the bed with head falling back over the edge of the bed. Then the drops can penetrate to the back and top of the nose cavity. In certain cases the doctor may prescribe a medicine to be taken internally to shrink the nose tissues. Similar to nose drops, these medicines don't hasten the cure of a cold but they may make the baby more comfortable, allowing for easier feeding and sleeping time.

Some parents and physicians nowadays don't believe in keeping a child in bed even when there's fever from uncomplicated colds, or keeping a child indoors until all signs of a cold are gone. From my personal experience, I'm inclined to believe that cold drafts on one part of the body may make a cold worse, even though it has been shown in experiments that chilling a person will not by itself produce a cold. So I prefer to keep a child cozy in a warm room, not hot, somewhere around 72 degrees, not necessarily tucked in bed but off the floor, away from windows from which there may be a cold downdraft.

What about diet during uncomplicated colds—whether or not there is fever? I feel that you can safely leave this to the children themselves. It has been traditional to say "feed a cold, starve a fever" and "force fluids," but I don't think it is sensible to push either of these sayings very far if they are not working. Different children react differently to the same infection and any child may react differently to different germs. Certainly it's sensible to offer the fluids that a child enjoys especially if he has lost his appetite for solid foods. Continue breast or formula feeding if acceptable to the baby. Water and fruit juices are good for small children. Carbonated drinks (even if the parents, as I, disapprove of carbonated drinks during health) may be given to older children.

Let children have their regular diet if they want it,

or any part of it. It's sometimes surprising what they still want during a cold. I'd also say don't push solids or fluids that don't appeal.

Many people (including myself) believe that they are less subject to colds if they keep the indoor temperature between 68 and 70 degrees. They may feel stuffed up when it goes above 72 degrees. But it's very easy in a heated house to gradually turn the heat up every time you feel slightly chilly. By watching a room thermometer regularly, you can train yourself to feel uncomfortable when the heat goes above 72 degrees rather than keeping it at 68 to 70 degrees.

It's also believed by people who have grown up with an emphasis on fresh air—as I was—that their resistance to catching colds is better when they spend some time outdoors each day when it is not raining. If there is any truth in this it must be particularly true of children who come home from school and immediately settle down in front of television.

Ear Infections

Infections of the ear in children are so common in the first few years and I have found that parents who are knowledgeable about these infections can manage them better and make their child feel more comfortable.

There are four regions to the ear. The external, visible ear gathers sounds and directs them into the external ear canal that ends at the ear drum. Behind the drum is the middle-ear chamber. That's where ear infections take place. The infection gets into the middle ear chamber through the Eustachian tube which runs from the back of the nose and throat into the middle ear chamber.

The Eustachian tube is intended to equalize the air pressure between the outside world and the middle ear chamber. If the congestion from a cold blocks the Eustachian tube, this produces a "stuffed up" feeling and impairs hearing to a degree.

The middle ear chamber also contains three tiny bones that carry the sound vibrations of the drum to a tiny spiral organ in the bone of the skull, the "inner ear." The sound vibrations are then changed into nerve impulses that go to the brain. It all sounds complicated—and it is. But all we are concerned with now is how an infection of the nose and throat may travel up the Eustachian tube, leaving it blocked. If the infection goes further it causes an accumulation of fluid or pus in the middle ear chamber which bulges the drum outward and is usually painful. This is the typical ear infection.

If an infection in the middle ear chamber persists and the pressure keeps increasing, the combination may cause a tiny rupture of the eardrum, which then drains pus through the external ear canal and out onto the external (visible) part of the ear.

Some children are more prone to ear infections than others, as some children have more colds. Younger children are, on the average, more susceptible than older ones, perhaps because their Eustachian tubes are shorter and more horizontal. Some children who are prone to colds and ear infections are found to be allergic to cows' milk and dairy products, which in some of these children may also cause stomach aches, diarrhea, and vomiting. They can be tested or taken off milk and all milk products for a trial.

In general babies who are breast-fed have fewer colds and ear infections because of partial immunity inherited through the mother's milk.

Children who play regularly with other children indoors, as in day-care centers or in nursery schools, are more apt to have colds and ear infections. This does not necessarily mean that they should avoid groups, but that it is a factor to be taken into account for the child who has frequent or chronic ear infections.

Ear infections are, next to colds, the most common infections in children and the most common reason for visits to the doctor. Seven out of ten children have at least one ear infection by the age of three years and a third of children have at least three infections. The frequency of ear infections goes down after the age of four.

Children who are exposed to tobacco smoke are more likely to have ear infections; so don't let anyone smoke around your children. This should be an added inducement for parents to give up smoking.

How do you tell if your child has an ear infection? A baby with an ear infection may have only one or several of the following symptoms. She may or may not have a fever. A baby may cry with pain or at least be fretful, particularly when lying down or eating because of the pressure of the fluid in the middle ear chamber. A baby may pull at her ear. An older child may actually complain of pain in the ear. A baby or child may lose her appetite. She may want to be held. And she may have no symptoms, other than a stuffy nose or occasional cough, if the infection is mild.

An ear infection usually (but not always) will show symptoms several days after a nose or throat infection starts. Hearing may be diminished with any ear infection, but it is not always obvious to parents or others. Usually normal hearing slowly returns after the infection subsides.

There are several first aid methods by which parents can attempt to relieve ear pain until they can consult their child's doctor.

- A hot moist towel may be applied to the face in the ear region, to relax the tissues in the ear. Younger children will tolerate less heat, older ones tolerate more.

- Warm sesame oil or olive oil drops may be dropped into the external ear canal provided the ear is not draining.

- You can prop the child's head on a pillow when she lies down, since this may relieve some of the pressure.

- If the ear is draining you can tuck a soft ball of absorbent cotton into the external (visible) ear, not deep into the ear canal.

When do you call the doctor? You should call the doctor when there is evident pain, when a baby tugs at her ear, when a child of two or more complains of ear pain, when a child who has had a cold seems to be somewhat deaf, or when an ear discharges.

Parents may feel guilty when a baby has been crying for several hours and they have begun to wonder if she has been spoiled, only to discover at the doctor's examination that she has an ear infection.

Until recently, antibiotics have been prescribed whenever an ear has become infected. Antibiotics are still prescribed when the infection is severe enough to cause distress. Now, however, many doctors believe in withholding antibiotics if the ear infection is mild, to see if the body can handle the infection.

The principal reason for withholding the use of antibiotics in mild infections, which the body can probably heal by itself, is to avoid the creation of strains of bacteria that are resistant to that particular antibiotic. In other words experience has shown that when an infection is treated with an antibiotic drug, a certain number of the bacteria, which are tougher than the rest, will survive. And their descendants will have that same ability to resist that particular antibiotic. Already there are several diseases for which the best antibiotics of the past have become useless, to the serious disadvantage of patients. Besides, if a mild ear infection gets worse, the doctor can always prescribe the antibiotics that he previously withheld. So it's important to let the doctor know when new symptoms develop even if the baby has been seen by the doctor. Usually the doctor will give you a list of symptoms for which to watch.

A few children continue to have one ear infection after another. The elimination of exposure to tobacco smoke, an evaluation for a possible allergy, and the certainty that the baby is not drinking from a bottle while lying on her back may prevent some of the infections. When these measures are not effective, a doctor may refer your child to an ear specialist, who may recommend the placement of a tiny plastic ear tube through a small incision in the drum.

Nowadays ear tubes are used less often than a few years ago. This is because they frequently come out too early and they can scar the eardrum. But they can bring real benefits for many children. You may want to consult with your child's doctor about an ear tube if other preventive methods have failed and ear infections continue to occur.

9

Stranger Anxiety

Stranger anxiety is an important and sometimes misunderstood event in the normal emotional development of all babies. Some psychologists have called it "eight-month anxiety" because it reaches a peak at about that age. I think of it as five-month anxiety because I saw it at that age in many babies—not all—in my pediatric office.

As early as one and two months, babies eye a stranger with interest and know the difference between a strange person and a familiar one. But at three and four months, they show definite pleasure when a familiar or unfamiliar person approaches, makes eye contact, nods the head, and makes sounds of greeting. They smile not only with their faces but with sudden wiggling of the whole body. In research studies, when an adult wears a blindfold as she approaches a baby, the baby does not respond. It seems that a social response occurs primarily to a visual connection with the eyes of another person. So you might say, half jokingly, that humans are at their maximum friendliness at three and four months of age. Never again will they trustingly accept everyone.

By five months they become more sophisticated in the sense of being more discriminating about whom they know and trust. I'll always remember the sequence of behavior of the typical five-month old infant during an office visit. He'll first be looking around at the surroundings with interest, waving his arms and legs, gurgling, as he lies on the examining table. But when I approach and begin the examination, he gradually becomes quiet—in movement and in sounds—as he eyes me, first very intently and then anxiously. After a couple of minutes his chin begins to pucker and quiver and he starts to wail. He may cry hard for twenty or thirty minutes and cannot be consoled, even by his mother. But he does not struggle or try to get away—he is physically passive.

The characteristics of stranger anxiety in the doctor's office after the age of a year is quite different from what I've been describing at five or ten months. This is an indication of how rapidly a child is changing in his emotional makeup at this period. Now when the doctor comes close, the one-year-old immediately tries to clamber to his feet and into his mother's arms as she stands beside the examining table. He tries to push himself and his mother away from the table. At the same time he sets up a noisy, angry crying. He buries his face in his mother's shoulder; but every once in a while he looks up suspiciously to see if the doctor is still there and then buries his face again and cries louder than ever.

As soon as the examination is over and the doctor backs away, the child promptly stops crying. Ten minutes later, while the adults are talking, he may even walk or creep over to the doctor, put his hands on the doctor's knee, or reach for the ear light, to figure out how it works.

There is nothing abnormal about the usual amount of stranger anxiety. There would be less manifestation of it if all adults showed more sense and sensitivity in approaching babies and young children. Some of them are so enthusiastic that they rush up close to a baby, without any preparation, and talk a blue streak of baby talk. Babies and young children need time to watch and evaluate a stranger before deciding whether it's a likable, dependable person. Even so, it's better for the adult not to get too close; let a child who is able to walk make the physical approach. At one and one-half-years-old, having decided that a certain stranger looks worth cultivating, after twenty minutes of observation, a child may fetch a toy and solemnly present it to the visitor. But in typical one-year style, he doesn't let go of it but takes it back. The visitor should feel flattered, though, even if she can't take the present home.

Stranger anxiety is more likely to occur with a first child, and particularly if the child has been cared for exclusively by a parent. The parent says to the doctor, "Lately he cries every time I leave the room; what can I do?" It may work if the parent will casually mention that she is going to the next room for a minute so that the child can crawl after her, or she can hum a tune while out of sight. This reminds the child that she doesn't disappear for good and that she'll probably be back. Playing games of peek-a-boo with a handkerchief is also a pleasant way to get the child past the stage of assuming that if the mother is out of sight it means she is gone forever. Psychologists call the new stage "permanence of objects," meaning that things and people continue to exist even when they are out of sight.

The mild form of bedtime anxiety, in the second year, is often accompanied by endless requests for going to the bathroom to urinate or for another drink of water—angling to keep the parent at bedside. If the parent is willing to play this game for hours, it confirms to some degree, the child's feeling that it will be dangerous to finally be left alone. Better for the parent to say cheerfully, matter-of-factly, "You have just been to do pee pee and you've just had a drink of water. Now it's time to lie down and go to sleep. Mommy will be in the next room."

A way to prevent these forms of mild anxiety or to help to hasten its cure is to have another person around the home occasionally, helping out with the baby, whether it's the father, a grandmother, a cleaning woman, a sitter. This reminds the baby that there are other people in the world besides the mother and that to have a familiar outsider in the home doesn't mean the mother is going away for good.

A more serious form of separation anxiety is when a

mother (or both parents) leave home
week or two (for example, to respond to
leaving the baby in the care of an unfam
if the mother decides to take a job withou
the baby for several weeks to being cared f   . unfamiliar person. Typically the child, of perhaps two or two
and one-half years, behaves well while the mother is
away, accepting the sitter and her care in a cooperative
spirit. But the evidence that the anxiety has been
intense and persistent all through the separation breaks
out when the mother returns. The child may cling to
her constantly or rush to hold onto her every time she
starts to leave the room. The clinging is usually worst at
bedtime. The child usually hangs onto the mother with
a grip of steel which can't be loosened, tries to climb
into the mother's arms, and cries frantically. If the
mother can detach herself, leaving the child in the crib
and heading for the door, the child may unhesitatingly
scramble over the side of the crib, though he had never
dared do this before, to chase after the mother.

The very visible anguish of a severe separation anxiety should warn parents about the risk of leaving a
child unexpectedly for several days with a stranger,
around the age of one and one-half to two and one-half
years. If the grandparents are thinking of offering the
parents a vacation of a couple of weeks, it would be wise
to get the baby familiar with a sitter or grandmother
over a two-week period before the parents take off. If
this isn't possible, the parents might consider taking
the baby along even though it will be less fun. If, on the

rents' return, the child acts panicky about being sep-
arated again, it's wise to avoid another separation, for
months if possible.

STRANGER ANXIETY:
COMMON SITUATIONS IN THE FIRST THREE YEARS

When a parent plans to return to work outside the home,
planning for the transition is always helpful. Engage a sitter
for two or three weeks in advance of the separation,
depending on how long it takes the child to accept the sitter
comfortably. Or, if the child will be going to a day-care
center, the mother should wait to go to work until the child
has made a good adjustment. This may take two or three
weeks. For if the child, after a week or two, gets hurt or
scared, he may demand his mother. And if it takes a long
time to find her, he may be very reluctant to return to
school the next day and thereafter. You may think I am
making too big an issue; but I have seen separation
anxieties that disrupted the family and upset the child for
months on end.

The treatment of a severe bedtime separation anxiety is
neither to try to ignore the panic nor to take the child back
into the living room or into the parent's bed. Either may
prolong the anxiety. The best course, in my experience, has
been for the parent to take the child back to his crib and then
for her to sit beside his crib, perhaps softly singing or
humming to him until he is fast asleep. If she tries to sneak
out before he is asleep he will jump up in alarm, and it will
take him longer the next time to settle down. It might take a
long time the first two or three nights for him to fall asleep,

---

but sooner or later he will take less and less time. In any case it is the only course I know that works.

These forms of separation anxiety are less likely to occur if the sitter is a familiar person or if one parent manages to get part of the day off to be with the child while the other parent is away, or if there is an older or younger sibling who will be at home. It's interesting that the anxiety will be less even if there is a younger baby in the home. The anxiety has little to do with whether the sibling can protect the anxious child. It's the familiarity of the person.

Another factor is the familiarity of the place. A young child is less apt to become anxious if he stays at home, rather than go to stay at the sitter's home.

Another expression of intense anxiety is when the child refuses to recognize his mother or father for a day or so after her return, gives her only a hard stare, as if he must punish a parent who has been so heartless as to abandon him. A shocking development in these cases in which the child manages to ignore the parent for several days is that, when he can ignore no longer, he is likely to unleash a barrage of pent-up anger, slapping or hitting the parent, perhaps using expressions of hatred. You can see how deep the hurt has gone.

If the anxiety and resentment can last for weeks and even months, you can see that it's worth all kinds of precautions to avoid such outcomes. If the mother has to go away on a trip, for example to care for a sick relative, it's much safer to take a child of one to three years along even though it may be inconvenient.

Get the child used to a relative or to a sitter who is regularly available; arrange for her to come in to take care of the child every week or two if you can possibly afford it. If your preference is family day care or group day care, consider enrolling him in a twice-a-week schedule and, if it is necessary, gradually build up to a five-times-a-week schedule.

By two years of age, the reaction to strangers is much less panicky, more controlled, unless a stranger insists on picking up the child without any time for becoming acquainted. We use the word shy for this mild anxiety at two years. The child is apt to hide behind the mother's skirt or pants while the mother chats with her friend, but eyes the friend carefully. If the friend is too forward, the child acts uncomfortable and tries to hide further.

I feel that sociability—the enjoyment of friend-ship—is so important that it's worthwhile for parents to invite friends to visit their home for the sake of a baby as much as for the pleasure of the adult. It is desirable to bring up all children prepared for easy sociability. After the first year, the first step is to bring any child to where other young children play, several times a week, as soon as she is able to walk. It could be a playground, or a home with a yard where young children and par-ents naturally congregate. If there is none in the neigh-borhood, I think it is worthwhile to search farther away. There may be a nearby nursery school or day-care group. It should be of high quality to be able to substi-tute for the mother for several hours a day, meaning a small group and a well-trained, kindly teacher.

I've concentrated on separation anxiety between one and one-half and three years of age. That doesn't mean that a child under one and one-half or over three years doesn't miss her parents if there is an unexpected separation. But the symptoms are likely to be different. Between half-a-year and one-and-a-half, a baby is likely to react by becoming withdrawn, less responsive to her parents, less active, and have a poor appetite. The personality change may last for a number of weeks. So the precautions in the way of accustoming the child to a relative or sitter are just as important.

After the age of three years children are much more sophisticated about what is going on around them. A child is more comfortable with strangers because of the inner growth of real sociability. He likes people and enjoys it when they show a liking for him. And his command of language—his understanding of it and his ability to use it—are much greater. So a parent who is about to go away for a week or two can explain this, with good expectation that it will be at least partly understood, and so that he can ask questions that will evoke meaningful explanations. The ability to communicate through the development of language helps him to manage the strong inner feelings that come from separation.

——10——

Transitional Objects

A child of two is following her mother from the parking lot into the supermarket sucking her thumb, with a faraway look on her face, dragging a dirty-looking rag which on closer inspection turns out to be an old, old tattered gray diaper. Her mother is embarrassed by this display but the child simply can't go out in public without the security that this ancient rag gives her.

"Transitional object" is a term given by a distinguished English pediatrician and psychoanalyst, D.W. Winnicott, M.D., to such everyday things as a stuffed animal or a special old diaper or blanket to which some young children become deeply, intensely attached. He used this solemn term for a technical reason: to indicate an object that, developmentally speaking, is midway between the thumb from which the baby gets pleasure in sucking and a conventional toy. But parents don't need to be particularly concerned with his theory. What they want to know is where such an attachment comes from, what it means, and whether or how it can be prevented or treated.

I lump these objects together for convenience and call them "comforters." Babies generally begin to form these attachments in the last half of the first year. Some are very intense and the child cannot go to sleep without it. Others are only moderate. In other cases the transitional object is a thumb to suck, the earlobe to stroke, or a lock of hair to twist.

In the first months of life, a baby's existence is entirely secure and pleasurable provided she doesn't have colic. She wakes because she is hungry, is promptly nursed at breast or bottle, and cradled in her mother's arm. She may gently feel her mother's skin or dress. Then she goes back to sleep again.

As the same child gets to be one, two, three, or four years of age, she will crave to get back to that blissful early infant state, whenever she is tired or hurt or anxious. She curls up, cuddles her stuffed animal or doll, or strokes her favorite blanket or diaper or her own earlobe or lock of hair. (If she's a thumb-sucker she will surely suck her thumb at such times.) She is trying to re-create the total security of the first weeks of life by stroking the object and sucking the thumb.

From observations of young children made during the child-rearing study at Western Reserve University School of Medicine from 1956 to 1967, we eventually came to several conclusions about transitional objects, all related to each other.

At the age of about six months babies begin to sense instinctively that they are individuals, that they have wishes of their own, and that they can and must learn to express and exercise them. If they don't, if they continue to do just what the parents expect or ask them to do, they would develop into zombies who were no use to themselves or others. Baby's first claims to independence are pathetically small. They want to hold their own bottles. They want to sit upright to be fed their solid food, not lie cradled in the mother's arm. In fact they don't want to lie down for any reason such as having their diapers changed. They struggle and cry each time they have to be put down, as if they had never before heard of such an indignity, such an insult. This beginning drive for a little independence from the mother is what endows the transitional object with its special value.

When children get to be a year and older their drive for independence is more dramatic. They learn to say *"No!"* even when a mother or father suggests some activity that they really love, like going to a park. Later, when they've been toilet trained, they may rebel against it. They turn firmly against vegetables that they accepted before. These revolts may seem insignificant to you and me, but it is very clear that once a child has gained a step in independence, she fights against giving it up again.

Despite the growing importance of independence,

when tired, hurt, or anxious children want to regress (retreat) back into the complete comfort and security of their earliest months. Their compromise is to regress back into actions that belonged to the early infant phase: to suck their thumb (instead of breast or bottle), to stroke a familiar fabric or object, with eyes closed. Yet they can retain their sense of independence by not appealing to their mother for help. So the transitional object retains the comforting aspects of the mother but has none of the masterful, bossy aspects that come with independence. Mother but not mother.

Why doesn't the baby, at times of fatigue or stress, turn back to the mother herself, to cuddle, stroke and nurse? I think it's because the child can't bear to give up the tiny sense of independence she has achieved, beginning at about six months. The drive for gradually increasing independence is perhaps the strongest drive of all during childhood. This drive is what gives the transitional object its special value.

Why does one baby develop a strong attachment to an object, another just a mild attachment, and a third no attachment at all? I've looked for the answer for many years, but I've not found it. Certainly the lack of a transitional object is not due to the absence of teddy bears and dolls; most babies have a cribful. Tense babies, relaxed babies, happy babies, tearful babies vary in their attachments—some have strong attachments, some have none, some have weak, transitory attachments.

Should parents try to break up these attachments? I don't think it can be done, and it's not worth the misery. The most that some parents, who dislike the appearance of a child lugging around such a dirty object, have accomplished is to have a rule, from one year onward, that the object must stay indoors or even in the child's room. But this takes a lot of vigilance on the part of parents, and may bring some unhappiness to the child. I don't think it's worth it.

Other parents ask if they should encourage an attachment. I don't think it can be done from my observations of children with a cribful of toy creatures who develop no attachment.

It's interesting that though the comforter is the baby's most precious possession (she must have it to go to sleep), she reserves the right to abuse it. At times when frustrated she will bang the animal or doll against the wall in a cold, cruel manner which may be a hint of the way she feels about her mother's or father's restrictions at certain moments.

For years, I wondered why many bottle-fed babies who were willing to take sips of milk from the cup at five months, as part of their mother's preparing them for weaning from bottle to cup, then turned adamantly against the cup at six, seven, or eight months. They'd turn their heads away or they'd let the mother pour the milk from the cup into their mouths but let it run right out again down their chins. Yet breast-fed babies made no such objection to milk from the cup.

Then I realized that when a mother gives her baby the bottle to hold and drink from, which a baby is happy to do at six or seven or eight months, the bottle itself becomes a transitional object (mother substitute) to which the baby becomes increasingly attached and doesn't want to give up. By contrast, breast-fed babies don't need a mother substitute when hungry and tired, because they have their real mothers right there. If parents want their baby off the bottle before two years, it's sensible not to give a bottle to drink in bed, so that it won't turn into a transitional object. (There are other reasons not to give a baby a bottle in bed; it encourages the development of dental cavities in the baby teeth and may cause recurrent bouts of ear infections.)

Similarly, a pacifier satisfies the sucking instinct in the earliest months. Most babies are willing to gradually give up the pacifier at three or four months; but by that time most mothers are so dependent on it as a soother that they keep popping it back in the baby's mouth each time she spits it out or whimpers. At six or seven months, a baby is beginning to sense her separateness, her need to decide some things for herself but also her need for a comforting mother substitute when tired or unhappy. The pacifier, if it is still being offered, becomes a transitional object to which the baby becomes increasingly attached.

I believe that the thumb itself, which is just a means of satisfying a strong sucking need in the earliest months, becomes a transitional object at around six or seven months, to which a baby becomes increasingly attached and may stay attached until four or five years of age, sometimes longer. To anticipate prolonged thumb-sucking, substitute a pacifier when the baby who tries to suck her thumb in the first week or two, and then let her give it up at three or four months.

Some parents who think that pacifier-sucking is more unattractive than thumb-sucking ask, "Why bother to substitute the pacifier for the thumb in the first week or two of life?" The main reason is that the pacifier is usually given up by about two years of age whereas thumb-sucking often persists until four or five years of age.

Of course many babies don't try to suck their thumb at all and there is no need for a pacifier in such cases—unless there is three-month baby colic which is mild enough to be soothed by a pacifier.

I don't believe that thumb-sucking can be permanently stopped by painting the thumb with bitter medicine or encasing the hands in mittens or by tying the wrists to the sides of the crib! It can only be stopped temporarily while the restraint is used. Besides, I think restraint is cruel. And it's unnecessary because the thumb-sucking will eventually stop anyway.

I think that the rhythmic habits that some babies develop in the last half of the first year—rolling the head from side to side, banging the head against the head of the crib, or bouncing against the back of an upholstered chair or sofa—are all transitional habits. They start at the same age as transitional objects, and the baby uses them to soothe herself when tired, hurt, or anxious. I think the baby is regressing back to earliest infancy when she was comforted by being rocked in some fashion. Transitional habits are repeated movements of the body that do not harm a child. When they occur intensely and for long periods of time, it may be a sign that the baby is bored and needs more attention. It is helpful to discuss it with the baby's doctor.

—11—

Sleep Problems

It's the middle of the night. The baby wakes and cries. Do you rush in, or let him cry? What is causing the baby to wake? Are you spoiling him if you go in every time he cries? On the other hand, he may have an earache and be sick, and really need you. How do parents decide?

If this is the first cry of the night, and if this is a baby who usually sleeps through the night, then you would want to go in and see about the baby. Maybe he needs his diaper changed or is unhappy about something else. He may be teething and even be running a low-grade fever. A lot would depend on the age and circumstances. It's not likely that you are spoiling your child unless it develops into a habit where he is continuously demanding your attention all during the night, and no one is getting any sleep.

Problems with sleep change with different ages even in the first two years. Although I make some generalizations, each child is unique and has his own special sleep needs. In general, a baby's pattern of sleep depends on his activity level when he is awake, his satisfaction with feedings and his parents' response to periods of awakening.

Newborns

A newborn baby will sleep most of the time except for feeding. In the first few months after birth, most babies sleep about 70 percent of the time. Except for awakenings for feeding, some babies seem to be asleep most of the other time! As long as a baby awakens, is alert and feeds vigorously, you don't have to worry about too much sleep. At six weeks of age, normal sleep periods vary from three to eleven hours—a good example of the tremendous variation among healthy babies.

Many parents ask about Sudden Infant Death Syndrome (SIDS) and wonder whether to put a baby on her stomach or her back. SIDS refers to an unexplained death of an infant in the first year of life (mostly in the first six months) during sleep. Not long ago, most babies were sleeping on their stomach and about one to two out of every one thousand infants died from SIDS. To put this another way, 998 out of 1000 infants were not at risk.

In 1992, the American Academy of Pediatrics recommended that babies should be placed on their backs to sleep. The recommendation was based on studies showing SIDS cases were reduced by 50 percent when babies who slept on their back were compared to those who slept on their stomach. At first doctors and parents were concerned that the babies might choke if they were on their backs, but this is not the case. Healthy babies will have a sufficient response and will be able to manage any spitting up.

I recommend the "back to sleep" position during the first year of life. In terms of preventing SIDS, this position is even better for a baby than sleeping on her side. A firm bed (not a water mattress or a supersoft mattress), breast-feeding, and an avoidance of smoking will also reduce a baby's risk for SIDS.

A baby can be in a room by herself, or you may want to put her in your own room for the first few months, when she needs more care. If you can easily hear her, then a separate room is fine. After about two to three months, you may want to move the baby out of your room and into her own. If she is sleeping through the night and needs less care, then she can easily be moved at two to three months. After six months, the baby gets used to the idea of sleeping in her parent's room and it gets harder to move her the older she is.

Six to Sixteen Months: Demanding and Walking

Some babies develop a resistance to going to sleep unless they are walked. They may have started out as a colicky baby in the first three months, then gradually got over the colic, but have become used to being walked and carried around until late at night. If you put the baby down, she instantly wakes and demands to be walked. The guilty parent gives in and continues to carry the baby, worried that she may still be in pain. It's best not to become a slave to your baby's demands to be carried for hours before going to bed. You should put her in her own bed. Make sure she is comfortable then turn out the light and leave. The first night she will scream for thirty minutes, the second night ten to twelve minutes, then by the third night she will get used to the idea and go to sleep without crying. It's hard for parents to do, but it will work most of the time if the parents are firm.

Naps: Six Months to Two Years

Most babies will want a nap in the midmorning and another in the afternoon. Each child is different. By the time they cut out one nap (usually the morning one), they will need a longer afternoon nap. This may happen when the baby is nine months, but for some babies who crave to sleep, both naps are important and they will continue to take two naps up to the age of two years. If the baby acts tired, you can put her in her crib and see if she will go to sleep. If she cuts out one nap, you may want to feed her earlier and put her to bed earlier at night so she makes up for the loss of a nap.

Co-sleeping:
Children Sleeping in the Parents' Bed

I have long advised not having children sleep with the parents. However, I realize now that 50 percent of some cultures in the United States practice co-sleeping; in fact, it is the preferred pattern of sleeping in most families throughout the world. There are advantages and disadvantages. I think that children are disturbed if they watch their parents during a sexual act. Child psychologists and psychiatrists agree that this can be disturbing and misunderstood by even the youngest child. Parents who choose to co-sleep with their children tell me that they find it easy to place the baby in another room during sexual activities. Another potential disadvantage to co-sleeping is that it may be more difficult to move a child to a separate bed or room when the child is older.

However, there are advantages to keeping the baby close so you don't have to get up to feed her. To the surprise of many doctors and parents, the amount of sleep time for baby and mother is increased among those who share a bed. Mothers actually report feeling as though they had a better night's sleep compared to awakening and going to another room to feed the baby. Not surprisingly, the frequency and amount of time breast-feeding is increased. And parents who prefer to sleep with their children say there is a closeness and bonding as they become aware of each others movements and sounds during brief periods of arousal from deeper sleep.

In families who choose to co-sleep, it is important that the parents do not smoke (at any time) and do not take medicines, other drugs, or alcohol that may cause heavy sedation. The bed should be firm (no water beds or couch) with a headboard that prevents the baby's head from slipping between the bed and wall. Avoid a heavy, bulky blanket and soft pillows.

Bedtime Rituals

I find it helpful to have a certain bedtime ritual when putting the baby or older child to sleep. You should be consistent about the bedtime, and make it early enough so that you have time for the going-to-bed ritual. You can start them with a bath, then dress them for bed, then read them a book. Some parents include a prayer, others teach their child a meditation at about age four years. The main thing is to keep this time as quiet and peaceful as possible. No TV or phone calls to interrupt. Your "manner" is also very important. A child going to bed may have fears of the dark, or of separation, and a calm reassuring tone of voice will give him trust and confidence that he is safe and can go to sleep with no fear.

Bottle in the Bed: Age Six to Twenty-four Months

You should avoid putting the baby to bed with a bottle for several reasons. First, the milk in the mouth can cause tooth decay. Also, the milk can run down the throat and into the ear canal, setting up a breeding ground for bacteria and causing an ear infection.

A third reason not to give the bottle at bedtime is because the baby will get used to it and later when you want her to give up the bottle, she will refuse to go to sleep without it. It's best to give the bottle while you are holding her, then put her to bed and avoid these problems.

Separation Anxiety: Six Months to Six Years

I think something should be mentioned here about a child's separation anxiety with relation to sleep. If a child is fearful of separation, or has other stresses going on in her life, such as a newborn baby in the family, an illness or death of a family member, a move, or a divorce of the parents, then you can certainly expect these anxieties to disturb her sleep. She may wake more often, begin wetting the bed after being dry for some time, or begin having nightmares. If these are disturbing enough, then you may want to consult your child's doctor, a developmental-behavioral pediatrician, or a child psychologist in order to understand the situation and best help you as your child goes through this stressful period.

— 12 —

Toilet Training

As I recount the various kinds of toilet training advice that I gave to my New York patients when I was in pediatric practice and that I wrote into different editions of *Baby and Child Care,* I struggled to find the best, the most surefire method, over a period of about forty years. It will illustrate the common hurdles to training young children to use the toilet successfully and that most babies are not ready to toilet train until after two years of age.

I was aware, from my own pediatric practice (which began in 1933) and from what my wife reported from conversations with other Central Park mothers, that many mothers in the 1930s tried to get started on bowel training in the first years of life. This was in line with the English tradition, brought to American cities by English nannies who wore blue capes and nurses' caps. They were hired by the wealthy to care for their children because they had such firm ideas about health and discipline. They believed that regularity of movements was the very foundation of health and that the habit of regularity should be established as early as possible in the first year by early toilet training. They prescribed supporting the baby on the potty at the same time of day every day. One Central Park mother would boast, "My baby hasn't had a dirty diaper since the age of six months." Another mother would counter, "Well, my baby has been clean since four months."

Careful analysis of these claims showed that it was really the mother who was trained—trained to catch the movement of a baby who had it at the same time of day. After a few weeks it becomes a conditioned reflex; when the baby felt the potty seat he pushed. But quite often in such a case the baby would rebel later—at fifteen or eighteen months. He would object to yielding control of this body function to his mother at this age when he was becoming more aware of his separateness and of his instinct to assert it. He would realize that this bowel movement (many parents call it "BM") is his own possession, as his hand or nose is his possession. If his mother gets too bossy about trying to control the timing or the disposal of the BM, he has the impulse to hold it inside or release it in some hidden place like his diaper or, if he has no diaper on, perhaps behind the sofa, any way that would keep it from becoming his mother's object to control.

The baby who was quite irregular during the first year was often difficult to "catch" and condition.

Usually the mother would give up after a shorter or longer effort. She'd try again in a few months. But if it was the second year by then, she was likely to run into the increasing resistance to yielding the BM. If the mother became more insistent, keeping the baby on the potty, the baby's resistance would grow enough to foil her. If she became grim, so would he. The conflict could sometimes last till three or four years of age and might, according to some psychiatrists, lead to excessively obstinate or compulsive character formation as they saw in some of their adult patients.

As a beginning pediatrician eager to help parents avoid emotional problems, I advised the first mothers who consulted me to avoid early and aggressive training efforts. I suggested, instead, starting at one year of age. This turned out to be poor advice, for some babies, because they were just getting to the stage of feeling more uncooperative or contradictory about yielding control to their mothers.

Why couldn't I have consulted other professionals? There were none at that time who had really studied the problem in infancy. There were the English nannies who had a strong prejudice for early training, the psychoanalysts who didn't see babies but who were vigorously opposed to early training because of what it might do to character, and the pediatrician who either had no opinion or who went along with early training because regularity of BMs was considered so important in those days.

Then, by coincidence, I was consulted by two mothers about other problems who said incidentally that they had stumbled on a perfect solution for toilet training. With their older children they had struggled long and hard to overcome vigorous resistance to training. When a third child came along they dreaded a repetition, and procrastinated. But by about two or two and one-fourth years these children, after observing their older siblings using the toilet, decided all by themselves to do the same and became trained not only for BMs but for bladder control! I enthusiastically passed this information on to mothers in my practice and in an early edition of *Baby and Child Care*. But I got grumpy responses from some mothers who complained that it hadn't worked for them at all. Next I recommended that parents begin training at about two years of age, and emphasized tactfulness and gentleness, so as not to stir up an uncooperative attitude. But if it happened, I suggested dropping training for a while. Some mothers still complained that their babies became resistant.

At that stage I moved to Cleveland and worked in the same department with child therapists who had been trained by Anna Freud. In general, their attitude was a no-nonsense one. They were direct and very clear in dealing with their child patients. Since I hadn't found that the advice I gave many of my own patients worked consistently, I took my cue from these child therapists and urged parents, once started on toilet training, not to give up but to persist in a firm but friendly manner. But still there were some failures.

Then in the mid 1970s, I read an article by T. Berry

Brazelton, a Cambridge, Massachusetts, pediatrician and friend who reported remarkable success with what was essentially self training in fifteen hundred consecutive patients of his own, between the ages of two and one-fourth and two and three-fourth years. He emphasized first that the baby should have reached the stage of being interested in putting objects in containers, which normally occurs in the second year. Then at one and one-half or two years he suggests that the parents buy a baby's toilet seat designed to fit over a potty on the floor, with a lid covering the opening. This is to be just the baby's own chair to sit on and play with for the next few weeks or months, with no suggestion of its BM-catching function. To repeat, this is to ensure that the baby feels that it is his very own plaything and that it is not a scheme of the parents to get his BM away from him.

Then, after the child has accepted the seat for weeks as his personal furniture, and he is between the ages of two and two and one-fourth years, the parent can casually turn the lid up, revealing the potty, and say—still quite casually—that the child can use it for BMs, just the way mommy and daddy use the big toilet seat. No more than that. No urging him to sit down and try it. If he does sit on it momentarily and then gets up, don't urge him to sit down again or to stay until he has a BM. The whole idea is to let the child have the feeling that he's in charge, that he can use the seat as he wishes. It's not part of the parent's scheme. A parent may show him how the parent or an older child deposits a BM in the big toilet.

Dr. Brazelton found that a great majority of his patients came to proudly use the seat between the ages of two and one-fourth and two and three-fourths years old. Furthermore they went on to urinate, enthusiastically, while sitting on the open seat, within a few days. The most remarkable result of all was that very few of the children became chronic bed-wetters.

I asked Dr. Brazelton why he thought my recommendation of self-training in the 1930s often failed to work, whereas his method which was much the same in spirit had been such a success in the 1970s. He said he thought the mothers of the 1930s and early 1940s really expected success in training within the first year and showed impatience to their babies when they wouldn't cooperate. But by the 1970s mothers had gotten over such ideas and were ready to wait with real patience until their children were over two years. I accept this explanation. In line with this interpretation is the fact that in England, the land of early training, bed-wetting in adulthood is one of the most common causes of rejection for the army.

13

Discipline and Temper Tantrums:

AN OPPORTUNITY FOR PARENT–CHILD COMMUNICATION AND LEARNING

Anger and Temper Tantrums

Is it anger when a newborn baby screams loudly with hunger? We can't ask her. We can only guess. I think it's close to anger—this feeling of red-faced fury over being hungry or crying with colic. But it's different from the anger of later childhood in that it's not directed at anyone in particular. The recognition of another person as distinct from oneself only begins in the middle of the first year.

For most children, it's between one and two years when temper tantrums appear. Children have become mature enough to have wishes and wills of their own, and they become angry when their mothers, fathers, or other caregivers interfere with their desires. But it's interesting that they are still not ready to direct their anger at their parents in the sense of hitting or biting, though at the same age they may bite another child who takes their toy. It's clear that there is still an inhibition against attacking the person who takes care of them. It's as if they've heard and take seriously the old proverb "Don't bite the hand that feeds you."

At the moment of a temper tantrum, they know who they are mad at all right, but they take it out on themselves by banging their heads against the floor.

I think it's wise to try to hold temper tantrums to a minimum, as long as you don't give in to unreasonable demands. The child's temperament will have some influence. Some one-year-olds, though they may be good-natured in other respects, have fiery tempers when frustrated, others are unusually obstinate and just hate to give in. These types are harder to deal with during this period of primitive feelings and minimal self-control.

The first principle is not to back down just because the child is raising a rumpus. For if you do, she'll catch on that tantrums get her what she wants and she may use them more and more deliberately.

On the other hand it's even more important that you not provoke the child unnecessarily and that when a tantrum comes, you help the child to get over it as soon as possible.

I'll always remember Mrs. Jenkins, the mother of one of my first pediatric patients. She called me in tears because her one-and-one-fourth-year-old son had "turned into a devil," doing the very opposite of whatever she asked. If she insisted, he'd throw a tantrum. I made a home visit and while we were talking, Ronnie toddled into the room. His mother said in a stern tone, "Don't touch the radio." (There was no TV then but Ronnie loved to twirl the knobs of the radio.) He had had no idea of touching the radio when he came into the room. He stood there looking her squarely in the eye for a full minute. She repeated the warning. Then slowly, slowly he moved sideways toward the radio.

Mrs. Jenkins feared from the first signs of his independence that she would lose control. In her anxiety, she brought on the very battle of wills that she dreaded. She raised issues that didn't need to be raised, shouldn't be raised. Ronnie, feeling challenged, asked himself: Am I a mouse or am I a self-respecting man? It's good that he had the impulse to ask for some rights and choices. He would have to have them to grow up. But his mother, being older and smarter, needed to be tactful, needed to be careful not to antagonize him with a lot of prohibitions, especially unnecessary ones.

If the radio was a problem, she should have set it on something high or locked it in a cabinet. In fact this is the age for "childproofing" the entire house, putting all dangerous objects, medicines, household cleaning products, and precious breakables safely out of reach. Breakables can be brought back at a later time, after the child has learned to respect requests. Jam books and current magazines so tight in bookshelves that they can't be pried loose. Leave pots, pans, blunt kitchen utensils where they can be taken out of cabinets, played with safely, and put back. (Taking out and putting back are fascinating activities and learning experiences at this age.) Empty cartons are as good as wagons for pushing around, and they don't nick the furniture.

If something dangerous or breakable gets left out by mistake and the child goes for it, distract him with something else. Have a music box or other machine that's used just for distraction and nothing else. There are a few things that can't be removed such as lamps on tables that you'll have to make "no-nos," perhaps by removing the child. Don't count on no-nos alone. Remove the object or the child and add no-no for emphasis.

How to help a child out of a tantrum has to be learned separately for each child. One child will keep trying and banging his head until his mother makes a peace gesture such as a suggestion that they go shopping or to a playground. Another child will sustain the tantrum as long as the parent stays in view but quiets down when left alone.

By three years and older, a child is much more consciously aware of what's going on between her and her parent. She has the language ability to ask for what she wants, to understand her parent who is explaining what can or can't be done. She will have developed trust—if it's justified—that her parent will give her what is reasonable, or have a reasonable explanation when she can't. So child anger is now no longer a half-blind explosion but comes out of a rational or rationalized indignation over feeling unfairly treated.

Physical Punishment

Almost all the parents with whom I've ever discussed this issue agree that they've had a strong impulse to spank their children at times, whether they believed in it or not. For example, when a small child breaks a precious china ornament that he has been told not to touch, or runs into the street where a car, with screeching brakes, just misses him. Or when a somewhat older child, say six or seven years, is picking meanly on her younger sister who has done nothing to deserve this, or calls her mother a stinker because she won't let her stay up to watch an exciting program on television. Or when an eleven-year-old has been caught stealing and then brazenly tries to lie out of it.

These are actions that the parents were taught were intolerable in their own childhoods so they promptly, automatically apply the same standards to their sons and daughters; and they tend to use the same discipline as their parents, whether it was spanking or deprivation or scolding or reasoning. In this way patterns tend to be passed down for generations.

The same persistence of beliefs occurs in other aspects of child-rearing. In some Native American tribes it is firmly believed (without proof) that baby's bones will not grow straight and strong unless they are tightly swaddled. In Turkey they assume that children are born without appetites and will starve unless forced to eat. In many South Pacific islands parents all agree that babies and small children should be pampered in all ways. In ancient Sparta it was believed that boys would only grow up with good characters if they were deprived of comforts and made to take hard exercise and cold baths.

In America, though many parents believe in physical punishment, we also have a worldwide reputation for indulging our children with possessions and privileges, such as the deluge of gifts on birthdays, Christmas and Chanukah—even an automobile (if the parents can afford it) at the sixteenth birthday or at graduation from high school.

Men in our country are more frequently in favor of physical punishment than women, particularly for their sons. I don't know whether this is because their hormones and genetic makeup have a different influence on their ideas. Or is it the way they were brought up to be tough, which really means to be afraid of weakness?

But can't you, as a parent, break away from the patterns with which you were raised, if you've come to disagree with them? Of course. It's being done fairly often, especially in modern times. But you have to have strong disapproval of your parents' methods in order to overcome the usual compulsion to do what was done to you.

There are really two roots to physical punishment. There is the belief that it's the right way to discipline for certain misbehavior. But more powerful is the wave of anger that sweeps over you when your child misbehaves; especially when there is an element of defiance in his act or in his attitude. He is challenging your authority, and there's a spasm of panic deep inside you that if you don't act quickly and forcefully, he might get the upper hand and you might lose some of your control permanently.

Even parents who disbelieve in physical punishment feel the anger when their child deliberately does wrong, and they feel the impulse to slap or strike. It's different when a child breaks an object or a rule by accident; then we excuse it without anger unless we are in a very irritable mood.

Most American parents have spanked their children when provoked. A majority believe that it's correct to spank at least occasionally; in fact they assume that you can't raise children properly without doing it, anymore than you could raise them without calories or vitamins.

It's interesting to learn, though, that in some parts of the world, it has never occurred to parents to slap or hit their children. I visited China to observe child care and schooling. I saw thousands of children in the care of parents or grandparents or teachers, in houses, in the street, and in schools, and I never saw a child being hit or even threatened with a blow. Yet children are generally well behaved there.

What convinced me most of all that spanking isn't necessary was getting to know dozens and dozens of families, through my pediatric practice, in which the children were never spanked and yet were cooperative, polite, and kind. In some of these families, the parents had not been physically punished either. In others, they were reacting to a conviction that the spankings they had received had had the wrong effect.

This raises the question whether physical punishment does any harm. It's obvious that when applied occasionally by loving parents it can't do much harm, because so many good Americans were brought up this way. But I don't think it's the ideal way to influence children, even in the best of families, and when used a lot, especially by irritable or harsh parents, its unfavorable effect is multiplied.

Physical punishment teaches children that "might makes right" and turns some of them into bullies. It leaves some sensitive children with a lasting resentment against their parents for having humiliated them in this way. It encourages, in some individuals, a feeling that violence is not really that bad, in a nation that has much more violence already—including murder, rape, wife and child abuse—than any other country in the world. It encourages people to think of war as a way to settle disputes, at a stage in history when a major war would destroy us all.

When a foreman in a shop or the manager of an office is not satisfied with the work of an individual, he does not come in shouting and swat the worker across the seat of the pants. He asks the person into his office where he explains what he wants. And most workers want to please. Children do too, though they are inexperienced and need a lot of guidance.

If a good friend is visiting you, and is watching TV after dinner instead of noticing that you are doing the dishes, you would not think of slapping her in the face. A quiet request for help will be all that is needed. You can use the same approach with your child if, from the beginning, you have shown respect and appreciation for her helpfulness.

I think physical punishment is a less effective and more risky form of control. It teaches that you can avoid the punishment if you can hide your mischief. In other words, wrong doing is all right as long as you don't get caught. Physical punishment teaches that when you've paid this penalty, the slate is clean; you can do wrong again if you are willing to pay again; some children are very brave in this way. They grin during the punishment.

But the most important reason of all for trying to avoid physical punishment, to my mind, is because it puts the main reason for good behavior on the fear of pain and on the fear of parent's anger. I think it's preferable for children to do the right thing because they love their parents and want to please them. Then, as they grow up, go to school, go to work, marry and raise a family, they'll carry over the same attitude of getting along in life by loving people, wanting to please them, wanting to cooperate with them.

As you can imagine, I don't believe in letting teachers or principals strike children in school. I realize that there are some out-of-control characters, especially in high school. But, I don't think you accomplish anything valuable or permanent with physical punishment. You only make them more resentful underneath, if not on the surface.

For if the staff of a school feels that it is all right to resort freely to physical punishment, they will, to some degree or another, stop trying to understand the causes of a student's misbehavior, stop trying to inspire him through special programs and projects that will make him feel that he is getting somewhere, like the rest of the class.

What about other forms of punishment, such as taking away a beloved bike for a day or so. To me, deprivation seems better than force and the indignity of blows. There should be advance warning about such a penalty and for which kinds of misbehavior it will be inflicted. The same applies to fines. Isolating a child ("time-out") who has gone out of control has been used effectively by many parents and in good nursery schools and day-care centers; but isolation should be used in a calm, friendly spirit, as a way of helping the child cool off, for his good, and not with shouts and blows.

But the best course, better than any form of punishment is to show children love and respect, beginning as an infant, and to set a good example. Then children's love of trustworthy, kind parents inspires them to look up to these parents and to want to grow up to be like them. I believe that children should behave well because they love and respect their parents, want to grow up to be like them, and want to be loved and respected by them.

When parents shout and hit, they diminish the love and respect and desire to imitate that children, by their nature, are ready to offer them. In the long run that makes the parents' job more difficult. If you complain that your children would never respond to anything as mild and quiet as a good example or a polite request, I'll admit that if they have been used to a noisier and rougher discipline, they will seem insensitive at first to gentler methods. But they will come around gradually. If you have been frequently spanking or otherwise punishing a child from early childhood, you can't expect him suddenly to begin behaving well just to win your love. It has been a battle for so long that both combatants have hardened their hearts. To soften hearts, the parent has to take the lead and avoid any harshness for not only weeks but months.

I've seen the transformation in a day-care center, for example, where a thick-skinned misbehaving child softens up and cooperates with a kind teacher after he slowly learns that he can trust her not to be hostile. One approach you can use to get the attention of a child who has learned insensitivity is to go to him immediately (rather than scold from across the room), put your arm around him and say quietly, "When you do that, it makes me unhappy. Please be kind!" By giving your child your full attention, showing affection, and speaking softly, you are proving that you want a change, are asking for cooperation, and are really hoping for a friendlier relationship. You shouldn't repeat this whole scene many times a day, but you can repeat it once a day. And you can be very careful not to hit or shout or show anger. Just look unhappy.

It's just as important to try to pay attention to

moments when the child is cooperative and friendly, and smile lovingly. Give him a compliment when he is halfway helpful or agreeable. Catch him at being good!

Today the great problems of the family, the nation, and the world—marital strife, spiraling divorce rates, violence in families, increasing crime rates, racial injustice, terrorism, wars, and the threat of nuclear annihilation—all these social ills are due in part to hardheartedness which develops early in life when children feel insufficiently secure, uncertain about being loved consistently, vulnerable to harshness.

If we can learn to guide our children through love and respect and kindness rather than punishment, all our problems will not disappear, but a major step toward a more peaceful and just world will have been taken.

Humiliation, Shame, and Guilt

Humiliation misses the mark as much as physical punishment I feel, and it is worse in that it lowers the child's self-esteem. To regularly lower a child's self-esteem really hurts his character in a permanent way. Commonly used examples are: "No one will like you if you act like that." "You're a lazy person and you won't get far in the job you chose."

Shaming a child is much the same as humiliating and has the same unfortunate effect on character. To control a child with shaming is to take away a fragment of his permanent self-esteem each time it is used. I've been amazed to see how sensitive a baby under a year can be to being laughed at; he may burst out crying. Ridicule is a form of shaming—or close to it—and it's too strong a method to use deliberately.

I've saved for the last the form of control that was used most often by my mother with her six children—fostering a strong sense of guilt. I imagine that she used guilt with the best of intentions, feeling that physical punishment was too crude, too physical; so she turned to the plane of morality.

Everyone should have a moderate sense of guilt, a conscience, to keep behaving themselves when no one in authority is around to remind them. Before it becomes your conscience, inside of you, in very early childhood, it is simply the actual voice of the parents telling you what is right and what is wrong. But gradually you absorb their teachings and they become part of your own beliefs or point of view. When you are tempted to misbehave, your own conscience, in imitation of your parents' teachings, reminds you that it would be wrong; you would feel uncomfortable until you put the temptation aside. But if you yield to the temptation, guilt makes you feel even more uncomfortable or anxious. A young child is afraid that if his parents discover his misdeed they will be angry and stop loving him. That fear of losing the parents' love and care is the sharpest, the most fundamental fear of early childhood. For a child instinctively dreads that he would be in mortal danger—of being lost, of having no protection, of having no one to comfort him, to feed him, to keep him warm.

I remember in later childhood dreading my parents' disapproval so intensely that I really wished they would substitute physical punishment, which would soon be over with, compared to guilt which would last all day or even several days.

I do believe that, even though the strong social conscience that I and my four sisters and my brother got from our mother's teachings was really valuable, the excessive conscience, the sense of guilt, the fear of offending people that we absorbed from her exclusive dependence on instilling guilt was a handicap that impaired our effectiveness at times. I remember when I landed a well paying summer job as "tutor companion" with the use of a car and lots of time off, mother said scornfully, "I'm ashamed of you, wanting to be a nurse-maid to a rich boy." This bothered me so much that I went back to the college employment bureau and asked for the most unpleasant job they had to offer.

The basic reason why I've pointed out the disadvantages of several types of discipline is because of their long lasting negative effects on character and motivation. In dealing with our adult friends or our fellow workers on the job, it never occurs to us to hit them, heap scorn or ridicule on them, shout at them or make them feel deeply guilty. We ask them in a friendly way to do what we want them to do, counting on their desire to please. Children are inexperienced and impulsive but are otherwise fundamentally the same as adults and can be treated in the same spirit.

—— 14 ——

Can You Spoil a Child?

The question whether a child is becoming spoiled most often hits the parents of a first baby between birth and three months of age. It's a period when many babies do a lot of fussing. The inexperienced parents have discovered that walking him around is as effective as anything in comforting him. A nursing will also work (at least for a while, even though a feeding has recently been given) or a pacifier. The parents want to comfort him; but sooner or later they begin to wonder and worry whether he may be getting spoiled, what with the frequent repetition of the fretful spells and their being stopped, at least for the time being, by carrying and walking.

I decided many years ago that since we really don't know what makes many babies fussy during their first three or four months, it's better to tell inexperienced parents, who have too many things to worry about anyway, not to worry about spoiling in that period but to do what works. Experienced parents come to that decision by themselves; they just say, "This baby is a fusser and needs more settling time." Another reason for not worrying about spoiling in the first three or four months is that it is fairly easy to cure. You say to the baby (he doesn't understand the words but he gets the tone) "I think you are getting spoiled. Your doctor says you probably don't have much indigestion or tension by this age and that it's all right to let you fuss for a little while when you've recently been fed. You and I know that you are not hungry. I'll be right in the next room." You say this not angrily but in an affectionate, reassuring tone. Hug him, lay him down and walk briskly to the living room. Your cheerful, self-confident manner reassures him that there is nothing seriously wrong and that you haven't stopped loving him.

Of course, if he cries louder and louder you pick him up and apply the old remedy for a couple of more weeks. The older he gets, beyond four or five months, the more likely it is that his fretting now has an element of habit and demandingness—it's not all discomfort. So you can be firmer in your declaration to him and in your decision to let him fuss for longer. I don't want to become more arbitrary than this in my advice or suggest that you should ignore your own feelings. But I have seen a few cases in which the baby has clearly gotten the upper hand, when he was of a very determined disposition and his mother was more yielding than average. He had learned to bully her. You could see his dominating nature also in his angry facial expression, until his mother gave in. Then he would promptly sweeten up.

Between eight and fifteen months, some babies who have been good about going to sleep quickly and sleeping soundly start waking in the middle of the night and crying. Some cases begin with a painful ear infection complicating a cold. In other cases we can guess (although there is no proof), it is pain from teething that wakes the child, especially if he is drooling, fretting, and biting objects, by day. First molars erupt at about fifteen months and they are more likely than earlier or later teeth to cause discomfort. The parent naturally hurries to pick the baby up and comfort him at this unusual happening. It may take an hour of walking, playing, singing, and perhaps a feeding to get him comfortable and sleepy again. He has appreciated all this company and fun. The next night—and the next—the waking and the parents' prompt response may be repeated. Whether or not the discomfort persists, the expectation of a good time may soon become a pleasant habit, at least in a minority of cases in my experience.

My advice is to be skeptical the second and third night of waking and let the baby fuss for a few minutes, to see if he will go back to sleep. If he cries harder and harder, I suggest not picking him up right away but sitting beside his crib in the dark, singing a lullaby, however long it takes to get him back to sleep. One more bit of advice. Keep the room he is in dark, especially if he sleeps in your room. Nothing makes a baby who wants to be picked up madder than to see his parents pretending to be asleep.

If you think this advice up to now is too severe, ignore it. A doctor sees the cases which have gone from bad to worse, not the ones which the parents have solved with indulgence, and this makes the doctor a little more strict.

In the age period after three years, I think of several varieties of spoiled behavior that bother me. One is the child who always puts up a disagreeable argument when asked to do something: "Why do I have to?" "None of my friends has to go to bed this early!," etc. How this begins and continues shows up when the parent, instead of indicating, however pleasantly, that of course she expects their child to cooperate, goes back to a novel, newspaper, or work from the office, as if she wonders whether perhaps she is expecting too much in asking for this particular form of cooperation.

I think that this parental hesitancy, in asking for cooperation or politeness, is the most common problem among conscientious, loving parents in America nowadays. I certainly don't remember any such hesitancy in my parents or the parents of my friends in the first part of this century, though I saw it by the time I started pediatric practice.

What has eroded so many parent's self-assurance in asking for reasonably good behavior? I think of several possible factors. First is the preoccupation with child psychology which has filled the shelves of bookstores and created a dozen magazines in the past thirty years.

Its impact has been to make some parents feel that only professionals know how to raise children and that parents are more apt to do wrong than right. It's the parents who themselves were raised in such a spirit that they doubted their competence, from childhood on. Parents allowed to acquire average self-esteem in childhood simply take it for granted that they'll know how to do it right, whether they incline toward strictness or leniency, and they can make either philosophy work.

Another factor, I suspect, is the mobility of young couples, who settle down far from the grandparents. So they can't turn to them easily for advice as they slowly acquire their own self-assurance, but are dependent on magazines and newspaper columnists who, too often, without meaning to, belittle or condescend to their parent readers.

Small families these days mean that many children grow up without the experience of caring for younger brothers and sisters, which is the easiest way to learn child care.

A common cause of spoiling, I think, is the guilt of mothers who have full-time, outside jobs, which, however essential for financial reasons, nevertheless make them feel they are neglecting their children. As a result they not only fail to ask for cooperation and politeness, they lavish gifts and other forms of indulgence on their children—give in to endless demands for reading more stories and treats, and permit rudeness and even abuse.

Such indulgences and inappropriate self-sacrifices on the part of parents do not work right in the long run. The parent, at least unconsciously, begins to resent the slavery to a tyrannical child and takes it out on the child in obvious or subtle ways—lack of enjoyment of the child's company, for instance. And underneath, the child knows that he is getting away with murder, feels guilty but cannot stop. He may behave worse and worse, as an unconscious way of asking for limits. He may become so selfish and demanding that he is unpopular with other children, too.

A mother or father has to recognize overindulgence and dare to become a parent who leads rather than submits, with or without the help of a counselor.

Index

AIDS (acquired immunodeficiency syndrome), 47
air, fresh, 89
allergy, 94
   to animal hair mattresses, 38
   breast milk and, 65
   to cow's milk and dairy products, 91
   to egg yolk, 62–63
   to wheat, 61
American Academy of Pediatrics, 47–48, 113
anger, 101, 108, 125–38
antibiotics, 93
anxiety:
   from guilt, 137–38
   separation, 97–98, 99, 103, 117, 118
   stranger, 95–103
   transitional objects and, 105, 107
appetite, loss of, 67–76
   during colds, 85, 88
   during ear infections, 92
   from separation anxiety, 103
   from teething, 7
applesauce, 61, 71

Baby and Child Care (Spock), 16
   on beginning solids, 61
   on circumcision, 44, 45, 47
   on infant feeding, 51
   popularity of, xiii
   on SIDS, 18
   7th edition of, xvi
   on toilet training, 119, 122
   on vegan diet, 66
back:
   infant on, 18–19, 80–81, 94, 109, 113–14, 117
   rubbing, 36
bacteria, 80, 84, 93, 118
bananas, 60–61, 71

LOOK FOR THE COMPANION VOLUME:

DR. SPOCK'S
THE SCHOOL YEARS

The Emotional and Social Development
of Children

Contents